# LOW FAT FAMILY COOKING

First published in Great Britain by Simon & Schuster UK Ltd, 2005
A Viacom Company

Copyright © this compilation WI Enterprises Ltd 2005. All rights reserved.

Simon & Schuster UK Ltd
Africa House
64–78 Kingsway
London
WC2B 6AH

This book is copyright under the Berne Convention.
No reproduction without permission.
All rights reserved.

The right of Margaret Foss to be identified as the Authors of this Work has been asserted by her in accordance with sections 77 and 78 of the Copyright, Designs and Patents Act, 1988.

3 5 7 9 10 8 6 4 2

Design: **Fiona Andreanelli**
Food photography: **Juliet Piddington**
Home economist: **Kim Morphew**
Stylist for food photography: **Helen Trent**
Copy editor: **Deborah Savage**
Proofreader: **Nicole Foster**
Printed and bound in China

ISBN 0 7432 5977 7

**Best-kept Secrets of the Women's Institute**

# LOW FAT FAMILY COOKING

Margaret Foss

SIMON & SCHUSTER
A VIACOM COMPANY

# ACKNOWLEDGEMENTS

It has been a pleasure to write this book but without the help of family and friends I would not have succeeded. Firstly, my family: Peter, my husband, who has always been there to help me with the computer, comment and even try testing some of the recipes; Andrew, our son, for sorting out the computer for us when we had a major problem and, with Jane, for testing some of the recipes; Nicola, our daughter, who gave me valued comments on aspects of the book and with the help of Andy, Alex and Joshua tested recipes. Then, my WI friends and colleagues who have tested many of the recipes and given honest opinions: Vera, Diana, Ann-Marie and Anne, all of whom have been my students for various courses; and Wanda, Sue and Fiona, from the Nottinghamshire WI Office.

**Thank you all.**

# CONTENTS

I was delighted to be asked to write a book on low fat cooking in a WI series on healthy eating. Enjoying food, both eating and cooking, and having been interested in healthy eating for many years, I am convinced that the best way to achieve a healthy diet is to eat meals that contain the whole range of food groups, of which fat is one.

We need to remember that it is 'low fat' which is the aim and not 'no fat', as a combination of the right fats is necessary to maintain a healthy diet. Lowering the fat content, and therefore the calorie content, of

# INTRODUCTION

food we enjoy means we can include all kinds of food in our meals, in moderation, and not have the cravings associated with 'diets'.

I am assuming that there are three main groups of readers who will be interested in this book: those who already realise that healthy eating is a way of life and are looking for new recipe ideas; those who need to lose weight, and know that lowering the fat content of food is an ideal way to do that; and those who wish to lower their cholesterol levels, which is achieved by reducing saturated fat – more of that later.

# FATS AND OILS – THE GOOD AND THE BAD

Fats are solid at room temperature, whereas oils remain liquid at that temperature. Both are very high in calories so lowering the fat/oil content of meals will automatically reduce their calorie content, which is ideal for those who need to reduce their weight. However, it is very important to include certain fats in the diet, while others should be restricted.

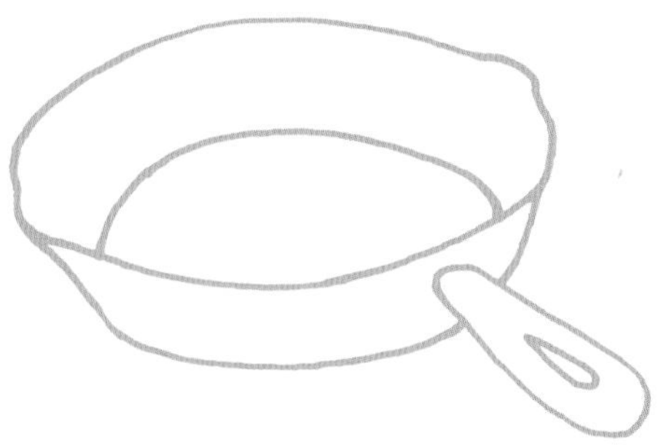

**POLYUNSATURATED FATS** Polyunsaturated fatty acids (PUFAS) contain substances that the body needs to function properly but which the body is unable to make on its own; they must be included in the diet. PUFAS can be divided into two groups: omega-3 and omega-6. It is quite easy to eat sufficient omega-6 fats, which are readily available in many spreads, but it takes a bit more effort to obtain enough omega-3 fats, particularly in a low fat diet; these fats help to protect against heart disease.

**MONO-UNSATURATED FATS** Mono-unsaturated fats are not essential to the body's maintenance but they do contain essential vitamins, though these are also available from other fats and oils. Mono-unsaturated fats do contain other substances which it is thought help protect the body against heart disease. There are no known adverse health effects from mono-unsaturated fats but of course they will cause weight gain if you eat too much of them.

**SATURATED FATS** Mostly of animal origin, these fats should be eaten as little as possible. They increase the level of cholesterol in the blood, causing blood to become 'sticky', which leads to narrowing of the arteries and, possibly, heart disease.

**TRANS-FATS** Trans-fats are created when oils are partially hardened to make them into spreads or margarines. These are as bad for the body as saturated fats and consumption of them should be minimised. (Some trans-fats occur naturally in certain foods of animal origin. These are not thought to be as bad as the artificially created ones.)

For those who wish to reduce their cholesterol levels it is important to replace saturated fats and trans-fats with unsaturated fats within a low fat diet. For this group of readers the best choice of savoury recipes would be poultry, fish and vegetarian (excluding or reducing the number of cheese dishes).

# FAT AND OIL CONTENT OF INGREDIENTS

Many of the ingredients in this book contain only a trace of fats/oils. As far as possible I have used the 'good' fats; where I have used 'bad' fats I have kept the quantity as small as possible. There follows a brief summary of the fats/oils used in this book. If you create your own recipes, or adapt some of these, this may help you decide which fats/oils to use. ('0-3' indicates the fats and oils that contain omega-3.)

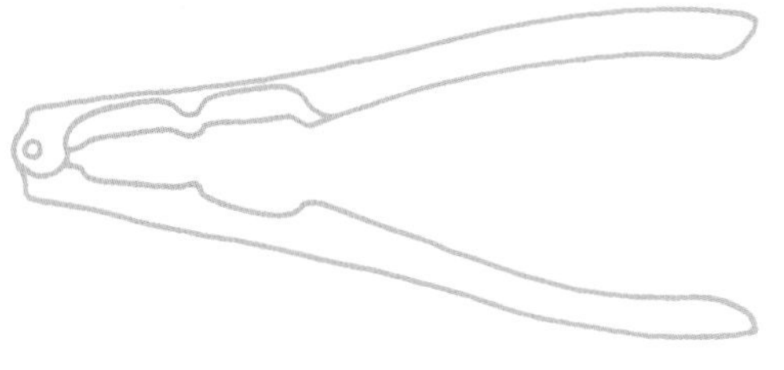

POLYUNSATURATED FATS:

**Rapeseed oil (0-3)**
**Olive oil**
**Sunflower oil**
**Nuts (apart from coconut, which is saturated; walnuts contain 0-3)**
**Seeds**
**Soya (0-3)**
**Oily fish, e.g., fresh tuna (0-3)**

MONO-UNSATURATED FATS:

**Rapeseed oil**
**Olive oil**
**Nuts**
**Seeds**

SATURATED FATS:

**Meat and poultry**
**Cheese**
**Cooking spreads**
**Dairy products**
**Eggs**

TRANS-FATS:

**Margarine**
**Cooking spreads**

In a diet which includes the whole range of foods we are bound to use some from the saturated and trans-fats lists, although these are the fats which should be kept to a minimum.

## SOFT SPREADS

Throughout the book you will see cross-references to this section. Soft spreads, based on sunflower or olive oil, are a much healthier option than margarine as they contain less of the 'bad' fats. However the proportion of unsaturated/saturated and trans-fats varies from one spread to another. Read pack labels to establish which contains the healthiest combination of fats – as well as considering which flavours you prefer. It is no good choosing the healthiest if you don't enjoy the taste! Soft spreads are those which contain between 55 per cent and 70 per cent total fat. They do not include block margarines.

Where soft spreads are specified, low fat spreads are unlikely to give such a good result. Low fat spreads are often not suitable for baking but I have found that they can be used in some recipes. For recipes that call for low fat spread, I used spreads with between 34 and 38 per cent total fat. Soft spreads could be used in place of these but, obviously, the fat content of the dish would be increased.

Spray oils in cans are useful for keeping down the fat content and can be used for greasing, 'roasting' and 'frying'.

## OTHER INGREDIENTS

Fat carries flavour, so lowering the fat content of a recipe immediately risks compromising the flavour. One way of coping with this loss of flavour is to add plenty of refined sugar or salt but this is not a healthy option. Refined sugar contains only 'empty' calories, having no other benefits than providing energy, with excess being converted into body fat. On average we already consume twice as much salt (sodium) as the body needs, leading to an increased risk of heart attacks and strokes. It is therefore better not to add salt at all in cooking or to use a salt substitute with reduced sodium, and to keep refined sugar levels as low as possible. The recipes in this book contain no added salt, apart from the bread recipes where salt is required for the yeast. You could use a salt substitute even in bread recipes.

To create tasty recipes while keeping sugar and salt levels down I have used well flavoured vegetables and fruit, herbs and spices. The benefits to health of eating five or more portions of vegetables and fruit every day are very well known and these ingredients have the added advantage of being naturally low in fat, so are ideal for a low fat diet.

## PORTION SIZE

How many does a recipe serve? How much you eat at one meal will depend upon several factors: age, activity levels, weather (we tend to eat less and drink more in very hot weather), the number of meals we eat in a day and how many courses we eat in a meal being the most obvious. The portions given in the recipes are a guide and are the size on which the nutritional figures are based.

## COOKING METHODS AND EQUIPMENT

It is not only what you cook but how you cook it that reduces the fat content of food. Avoid frying and roasting, unless following the methods given in this book. Instead try grilling, baking, steaming, dry- and stir-frying. Make use of any low fat cooking equipment you have. In many of the recipes it would be appropriate to use a 'healthy eating grill', slow-cooker or microwave if you have one; just follow the manufacturer's instructions for that part of the recipe.

I have had a loyal team of testers for these recipes, and it has been particularly useful to read their comments when their equipment has been different from mine. We found that timings for certain processes varied, depending on the material from which the equipment was made. This was particularly noticeable with saucepans and frying pans. When you are trying a recipe for the first time, do keep a more careful eye than usual on what you are cooking! Also, keep to either metric or imperial measurements for the best results and don't use a mixture of the two.

These recipes have all been tried and tested by others, so you can try them with confidence – I hope you enjoy both cooking and tasting them.

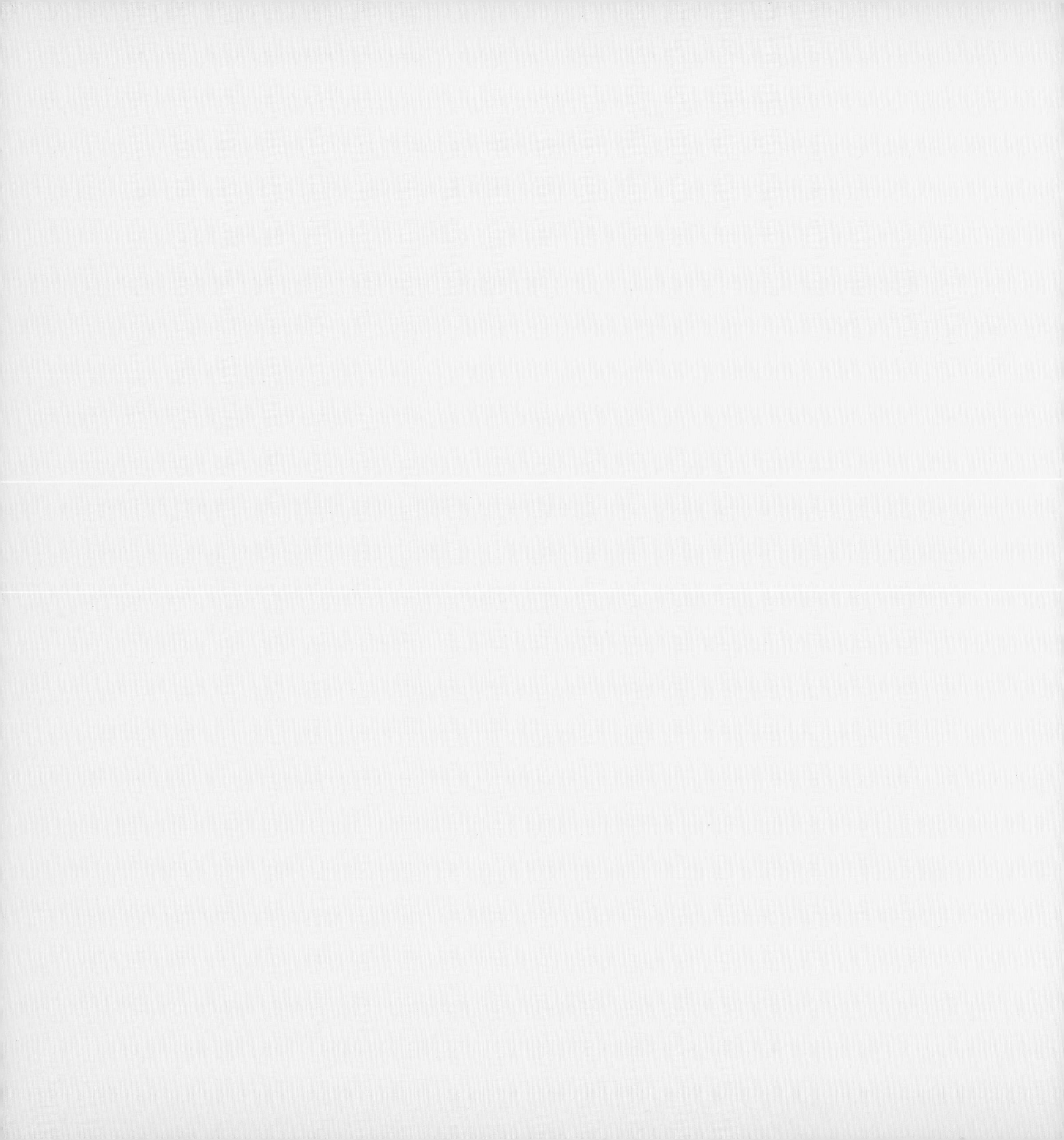

Warming, colourful and flavoursome, soups need very little added fat and can be eaten at the start of a meal or as a hearty snack served with bread. Three of the soups given here are fairly thick; to make them thinner for a starter just add extra stock. I always use the best available stock as it adds to the flavour of the soup.

# SOUPS & STARTERS

Salads and vegetables make ideal starters as they are not too filling, contain little fat and whet the appetite. All these recipes could be served as light lunches; just increase the quantities.

All the soups and most of the starters can be prepared in advance, good news for when you entertain!

SERVES: 6
PREPARATION & COOKING TIME:
35 minutes + 30 minutes cooking
FREEZING: recommended

# TOMATO & PEPPER SOUP

This **brightly coloured** soup can be made all year round. Use fresh tomatoes in the late summer and autumn, when the flavours are at their best, and canned, chopped tomatoes the rest of the year.

PER SERVING: 55 calories, 1 g fat

**1 red pepper, cored, de-seeded and halved**
**1 yellow pepper, cored, de-seeded and halved**
**1 green pepper, cored, de-seeded and halved**
**spray oil**
**1 onion, sliced**
**500 g (1 lb 2 oz) *ripe* tomatoes, peeled, de-seeded and chopped or a 400 g can of chopped tomatoes**
**600 ml (1 pint) fresh vegetable stock**
**1½ teaspoons dried mixed Italian herbs**
**2 teaspoons sugar**
**1 tablespoon concentrated tomato purée**
**1 tablespoon lemon juice**
**freshly ground black pepper**
**2 tablespoons natural low fat yogurt, to garnish**

1. Heat the grill to high. Line a grill pan with foil and place the pepper halves on it. Grill the peppers until the skins are charred. Remove from the grill pan and place in a polythene bag for 5 minutes.
2. Spray the base of a saucepan (about 3 sprays) with oil. Add the onion and stir-fry for 3 minutes.
3. Peel the skins from the peppers and discard them. Chop the pepper flesh and add to the onion.
4. Add the tomatoes, stock, herbs, sugar, tomato purée and lemon juice, bring to the boil and then simmer for 30 minutes.
5. Allow to cool a little and then blend in a liquidiser.
6. Reheat and adjust the seasoning with pepper, to taste. Garnish with a swirl of yogurt.

SERVES: 4
PREPARATION & COOKING TIME: 35 minutes
FREEZING: recommended

# SWEET POTATO & ONION SOUP

We first tasted this soup in an **inn in Norfolk** and liked it so much that I came home to try to reproduce the recipe. This is my version!

PER SERVING: 126 calories, 1 g fat

**500 g (1 lb 2 oz) sweet potatoes, peeled and chopped roughly**
**1 large onion, sliced**
**600 ml (1 pint) good chicken or vegetable stock**
**freshly ground black pepper**

1. Put the sweet potatoes in a saucepan. Add the onion but reserve a few slices.
2. Add half the stock to the vegetables. Bring to the boil, covered, and then simmer until tender.
3. In a small pan, cook the few onion slices in a little water.
4. Allow the soup to cool a little, then add the remaining stock. Liquidise the soup. Reheat and adjust the seasoning with pepper to taste.
5. Serve garnished with the separately cooked onion slices.

SERVES: 3
PREPARATION & COOKING TIME:
20 minutes + 25 minutes cooking
FREEZING: not recommended

# FRUITY RICE SALAD

Brown rice has a **lovely nutty flavour, which complements the fruit** in this starter. It would also be suitable as a lunch dish, served with slices of chicken.

PER SERVING: 256 calories, 5 g fat

**110 g (4 oz) long-grain brown rice**
**1 eating apple**
**2 teaspoons lemon juice**
**1 orange**
**6 ready-to-eat prunes, quartered**
**2 teaspoons sunflower seeds, toasted**
**1–2 tablespoons low fat natural yogurt**
**freshly ground black pepper**
**lettuce leaves, e.g. Little Gem, to serve**
**2 teaspoons walnut pieces, to garnish**

1. Cook the rice according to the packet instructions, until it is tender but still has a little bite to it, about 25 minutes. Drain, rinse in cold water and drain again.
2. Core and slice the apple and then halve across the slices. Toss the slices in lemon juice to prevent browning.
3. Peel and segment the orange, removing as much pith as possible and retaining any juice.
4. Toss together the rice, fruit and sunflower seeds.
5. Make the dressing by combining the yogurt and reserved orange juice. Season to taste with pepper.
6. Just before serving, toss the salad in the dressing.
7. Serve on lettuce leaves, garnished with the walnut pieces.

SERVES: 4
PREPARATION & COOKING TIME: 35 minutes
FREEZING: recommended

# CARROT & PARSNIP SOUP

The distinctive flavours of carrot and parsnip combine well to make this **colourful and warming** soup.

PER SERVING: 80 calories, 1 g fat

**300 g (10½ oz) parsnips, chopped**
**300 g (10½ oz) carrots, chopped roughly**
**1 onion, chopped**
**600 ml (1 pint) good chicken or vegetable stock**
**¼–½ teaspoon freshly grated nutmeg**
**freshly ground black pepper**
**fresh parsley, to garnish**

1. Remove the core from the parsnips if they are very woody.
2. Place all the vegetables in a saucepan and pour half the stock over them. Cover with a lid.
3. Bring to the boil and then simmer until tender.
4. Add the remaining stock and, when cool enough, liquidise the soup.
5. Reheat, taste and season with the nutmeg and pepper.
6. Serve, garnished with fresh parsley leaves.

SERVES: 4
PREPARATION & COOKING TIME:
20 minutes + 30 minutes cooking
FREEZING: recommended

# BUTTERNUT SQUASH SOUP

An **unusual** soup which is really **easy to make**. To vary the flavour, add a tablespoon of chopped fresh herbs or a teaspoon of dried mixed herbs such as *herbes de Provence* in place of the nutmeg.

PER SERVING: 119 calories, 2 g fat

**1 butternut squash, peeled and de-seeded**
**2 onions, chopped**
**1 large leek, chopped**
**2 large celery sticks, chopped**
**425 ml (¾ pint) vegetable stock**
**½ teaspoon freshly grated nutmeg**
**freshly ground black pepper**

1. Chop the butternut squash into pieces of about 2.5 cm (1 inch) square.
2. Put all the vegetables into a large saucepan with 300 ml (½ pint) of the stock. Cover with the lid.
3. Bring to the boil and then simmer for 20–30 minutes, until all the vegetables are tender.
4. Add the remaining stock and, when cool enough, liquidise the soup.
5. Reheat and season to taste with nutmeg and pepper.

SERVES: 4
PREPARATION & COOKING TIME:
30 minutes + 1 hour chilling
FREEZING: not recommended

PER SERVING: 31 calories, 1 g fat

Serve this **lovely coloured pâté with thinly sliced toast** or use as a dip with crudités. Half-fat cream cheese can be used instead of the yogurt; it will give a richer pâté but triple the fat content.

# GOLDEN VEGETABLE PÂTÉ

**1 onion, sliced**
**1–2 garlic cloves**
**125 g (4½ oz) carrot, chopped**
**125 g (4½ oz) swede, chopped**
**1–2 teaspoons grated orange zest**
**1 ½ tablespoons light Greek yogurt**
**½ teaspoon ground coriander**
**freshly grated nutmeg**
**freshly ground black pepper**

1. Place the onion in a small, heavy-based saucepan and cover with the lid. Heat over a gentle heat for 10 minutes, shaking the pan occasionally until the onion starts to soften but not brown.
2. Add the garlic, carrots and swede to the pan, with enough boiling water to cook them. Simmer until the vegetables are tender. If possible evaporate off any remaining water; if too much is left to do this, pour it off and retain it to use as stock. Cool the vegetables.
3. Add the orange zest, yogurt and the coriander to the vegetables; process in a small blender or liquidise until smooth. Season to taste with nutmeg and pepper. Chill for at least an hour before serving.

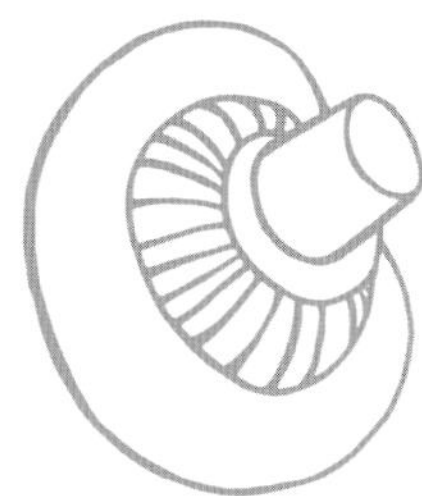
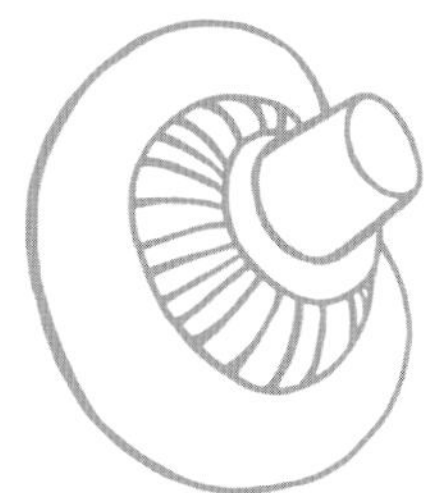
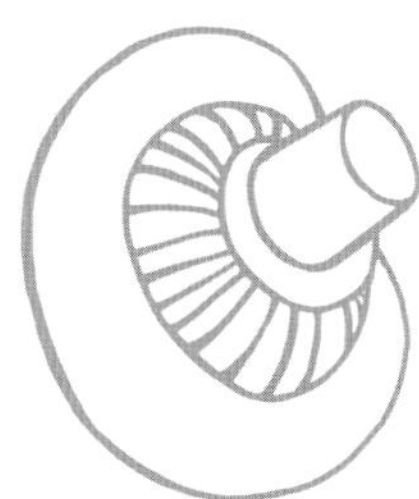

SERVES: 4
PREPARATION & COOKING TIME: 30 minutes soaking + 20 minutes + chilling
FREEZING: not recommended

PER SERVING: 78 calories, 6 g fat

The dried mushrooms give this dark pâté a **wonderfully strong flavour**. Serve with fingers of toast.

# MUSHROOM PÂTÉ

**40 g packet of porcini mushrooms**
**spray oil**
**125 g (4½ oz) chestnut mushrooms, wiped and sliced**
**1 garlic clove, chopped**
**110 g (4 oz) light cream cheese**
**2 teaspoons lemon juice**
**freshly ground black pepper**
**a few drops of Tabasco sauce**
**freshly grated nutmeg**
**chopped fresh parsley, to garnish**

1. Soak the porcini mushrooms in 100 ml (3 ½ fl oz) hot water for at least 30 minutes.
2. Coat the base of a frying pan with about 4 sprays of oil. Heat the oil and stir-fry the chestnut mushrooms with the garlic for 1 minute. Remove from the pan.
3. Fry the soaked mushrooms for 1 minute to dry them.
4. Put the cheese and lemon juice into a small processor or liquidiser. Add most of the chestnut mushrooms, reserving a few for garnish, the porcini mushrooms and the garlic. Process until the mixture is smooth.
5. Season to taste with black pepper, Tabasco and nutmeg. Spoon into a serving dish and chill.
6. Remove from the refrigerator 30 minutes before serving, to allow the flavours to develop.
7. Serve garnished with the reserved sliced mushrooms and a little chopped parsley.

# PRAWN & PAPAYA SALAD

SERVES: 2
PREPARATION & COOKING TIME:
30 minutes soaking + 20 minutes
FREEZING: not recommended

PER SERVING: 123 calories, 2 g fat

Papaya, also known as paw-paw, has a creamy but firm flesh, similar in texture to mango. However, it is much less sweet and complements the flavour of the prawns when tossed in this **mildly spiced tomato dressing**. The skins of the papaya can be used as shells in which to serve the salad.

**150 g (5½ oz) cooked king prawns**
**1 papaya, halved lengthways**

FOR THE DRESSING:
**4 tablespoons light Greek yogurt**
**1½ teaspoons tomato purée**
**1½ teaspoons lemon or lime juice**
**about 1 teaspoon sweet chilli sauce**
**freshly ground black pepper (optional)**
**watercress, trimmed of coarse stalks, to garnish**

1. Soak the prawns in cold water for about 30 minutes to remove some of the salt. Drain and dry well.
2. Remove and discard the black papaya seeds. Remove the flesh from the skin using a melon baller or a teaspoon. If using a teaspoon cut the flesh into evenly sized pieces of about 1 cm (½-inch) square. Mix the papaya with the prawns.
3. Prepare the dressing: combine the yogurt, tomato purée, citrus juice and chilli sauce to taste. Taste and adjust the seasoning, adding pepper if required.
4. Just before serving, stir the prawns and papaya into the dressing and then spoon into the papaya shells. Use a little watercress to garnish the plates.

VARIATION: If you prefer to serve the salad without the papaya shells, strew individual serving plates with mild-flavoured lettuce leaves, such as Little Gem, Oak Leaf and Apollo, and watercress. This could serve three, making a still lighter starter.

SERVES: 6
PREPARATION & COOKING TIME: 50 minutes
FREEZING: not recommended

# BABY AUBERGINE & COURGETTE PLATTER

In this **sophisticated** starter, **grilled baby aubergines and courgettes are complemented by a tasty smoked haddock mixture**. There is also a vegetarian variation, in which a richly flavoured red pepper sauce replaces the smoked haddock. You could even serve a mixture of both sauces, remembering to halve the quantity of each one. Both sauces can be made in advance and then reheated when needed.

The vegetables could be steamed instead of grilled; the cooking time will still be 8–10 minutes.

PER SERVING: 88 calories, 2 g fat

**5–6 baby aubergines, halved lengthways**
**1 tablespoon lemon juice**
**1 quantity filling only, Smoked Haddock Lasagne (see page 42)**
**3 courgettes about 17 cm (6½ inches) long**
**spray oil**
**2 tablespoons chopped fresh parsley**
**small green lettuce or rocket leaves, to garnish**

1. Brush the aubergines with the lemon juice to prevent browning.
2. Prepare the smoked haddock lasagne filling as described in steps 2–4 on page 42.
3. Trim the courgettes, cut them in half lengthways and then cut each half into three widthways.
4. Heat the grill to medium.
5. Place the aubergines and courgettes on a grill pan lined with foil, cut-side up, and spray with oil. Place under the grill and cook for 3–5 minutes, until golden.
6. Turn the vegetables over and spray again with the oil. Replace under the grill and cook for a further 3–5 minutes, until tender. The courgettes may cook more quickly than the aubergines; in this case, turn the courgettes first and remove them as soon as they are cooked, continuing to cook the aubergines.
7. Place the vegetables on a warmed platter and spoon the smoked haddock mixture on top.
8. Sprinkle with the parsley and garnish with lettuce or rocket leaves between the vegetables.

VARIATION: For a vegetarian filling, use 1 quantity of Red Pepper Sauce (see page 54). If the sauce still has a lot of free liquid, reduce it by boiling, uncovered, until it is thick but not sticking to the base of the pan. Blend ½ tablespoon of arrowroot with 2 tablespoons port, red wine or water and stir it into the sauce. Bring to the boil and simmer for 1 minute. Keep warm. Garnish with fresh basil leaves instead of lettuce or rocket.

SERVES: 6
PREPARATION & COOKING TIME:
25 minutes + 20 minutes cooking
FREEZING: recommended

# CHICKEN TIMBALES

Serve these **little timbales with mixed salad leaves**. The timbales are lightly flavoured; if you prefer a stronger flavour replace the tomatoes with a small red pepper, de-seeded and finely chopped. Made into four timbales, these quantities would make a **great light lunch dish**, served with salad and new potatoes.

PER SERVING: 69 calories, 2 g fat

**375 g (13 oz) skinless chicken fillets or pieces**
**6 mini plum tomatoes, skinned**
**4 spring onions, chopped finely**
**1–2 celery sticks (depending on size), chopped finely**
**1 teaspoon grated lemon zest**
**1 tablespoon chopped fresh parsley**
**1 teaspoon Worcestershire sauce**
**½–1 teaspoon mustard**
**1 egg, beaten**
**freshly ground black pepper**
**rocket leaves or fresh dill sprigs, to garnish**

1. Preheat the oven to Gas Mark 4/electric oven 180°C/fan oven 160°C. Lightly grease six small ovenproof ramekin dishes (or cups).
2. Dice the chicken into pieces of 5–10 mm (¼–½ inch) and place in a bowl.
3. Chop the tomatoes into small pieces, discarding any juice that comes out. Add to the chicken.
4. Stir the spring onions, celery, lemon zest, parsley and Worcestershire sauce into the chicken mixture.
5. Beat the mustard into the beaten egg (judge the amount depending on the strength of the mustard). Add this to the chicken mixture. Season with the pepper. Stir to mix well.
6. Spoon into the ramekin dishes, cover with foil and place the dishes on a baking sheet.
7. Bake for about 20 minutes until the mixture has set and any chicken juices are clear. Remove from the oven and allow to stand for 5 minutes, covered. Carefully tip off any juices. Turn out on to individual serving plates and garnish with the rocket or dill.

The very word 'vegetarian' suggests healthy eating, as we know how good vegetables are for us. Using good-quality vegetables ensures a true flavour and so it should not be necessary to add a lot of fat to increase the flavour. One of the keys to a healthy vegetarian diet is to vary the ingredients used across a wide range to ensure you eat

# VEGETARIAN MAIN COURSE

enough protein. You can easily do this by choosing a mixture of pulses (peas and beans) and grains (such as bread, rice and pasta), with a smaller amount of nuts and seeds throughout the day.

So many people enjoy vegetarian food that, even if you are not vegetarian, I hope you will enjoy making some of the recipes in this section.

SERVES: 4
PREPARATION & COOKING TIME: 50 minutes
FREEZING: recommended (freeze the stew and couscous separately)

# MOROCCAN-STYLE CHICK-PEA STEW WITH COUSCOUS

Your choice of fruit adds interest to the couscous, complementing the **lightly spiced vegetable and chick-pea stew.**

PER SERVING: 358 calories, 7 g fat

**1 onion, sliced**
**1 red pepper, halved and de-seeded**
**1 yellow pepper, halved and de-seeded**
**1 green pepper, halved and de-seeded**
**2 garlic cloves, chopped finely**
**½ small fresh chilli, de-seeded and chopped finely**
**2 tablespoons tomato purée**
**½ teaspoon ground cumin**
**1 aubergine, trimmed and diced**
**1 courgette, trimmed, halved lengthways and sliced into 5 mm (¼ inch) pieces**
**410 g can of chick-peas in water, drained**
**about 300 ml (½ pint) vegetable stock**
**freshly ground black pepper**
**225 g (8 oz) couscous**
**85 g (3 oz) dates or lexia raisins, or use half dates and half ready-to-eat dried apricots, chopped**
**300 ml (½ pint) boiling water**
**4 tablespoons chopped fresh lemon balm or parsley**
**25 g (1 oz) pine nuts, toasted**

1. Put the onion slices in a small, heavy-based pan. Place on a low heat and cook, covered, for about 15 minutes, until softened.
2. Heat the grill. Lay the pepper halves, skin-sides up on a foil-lined grill pan and grill until the skins are blackened.
3. Put the peppers into a polythene bag or a basin covered with cling film and leave to cool.
4. Stir the garlic, chilli, tomato purée and cumin into the onion and cook for 2 minutes; remove from the heat.
5. Remove the skin from the peppers and slice into strips.
6. Transfer the onion mixture to a larger pan. Add the peppers, aubergine and courgette to this and stir well.
7. Add the chick-peas and stock. Bring to the boil, cover and simmer for 20 minutes, adding more stock if necessary.
8. Meanwhile, prepare the couscous. Mix the couscous and chosen fruit in a bowl and then stir in the boiling water. Cover and leave to soak for 10 minutes, until the water is absorbed and the couscous soft. The flavour is fairly bland, to balance the spicy stew. After 10 minutes, separate the grains with a fork.
9. Stir the lemon balm or parsley through the stew.
10. To serve, form a ring with the couscous and pour the stew in the middle. Scatter the pine nuts over the couscous.

COOK'S TIP: Lexia raisins are a type of raisin grown in Australia. They are available in many supermarkets and in health-food stores.

SERVES: 6
PREPARATION & COOKING TIME:
20 minutes + 1 ½–1 ¾ hours cooking
FREEZING: recommended

# BEAN & VEGETABLE HOTPOT

**Easy to make**, this colourful dish is good with Herby Dumplings (page 50), Naan Breads (page 56), rice or a jacket potato. If you wish, add 4 tablespoons of port with the sweetcorn. The flavour is even better if stored in the refrigerator for a day or two before eating.

PER SERVING: 138 calories, 2 g fat

**1 small aubergine, sliced and larger slices halved**
**1 tablespoon lemon juice**
**2 garlic cloves, chopped finely**
**1 large onion, chopped**
**1 red pepper, de-seeded and chopped into 5–10 mm (¼–½-inch) pieces**
**1 yellow pepper, de-seeded and chopped into 5–10 mm (¼–½ -inch) pieces**
**1 green pepper, de-seeded and chopped into 5–10 mm (¼–½ -inch) pieces**
**400 g can of red kidney beans in water, drained well, rinsed and drained again**
**2 x 400 g cans of chopped tomatoes with herbs**
**2 tablespoons fresh or 2 teaspoons dried basil or similar herb (increase this if you can't get tomatoes with herbs)**
**2 courgettes, sliced**
**225 g (8 oz) frozen sweetcorn kernels**
**freshly ground black pepper**

1. Brush the aubergine slices with the lemon juice to prevent browning.
2. Put the garlic, onion, peppers, beans, tomatoes and herbs into a large pan.
3. Cover, bring to the boil and simmer for 30 minutes, until the vegetables are beginning to soften.
4. Add the courgettes and aubergine, bring back to the boil and simmer for a further 45–60 minutes.
5. Add the sweetcorn, bring back to the boil and simmer for 5 minutes. Season to taste with black pepper.

SERVES: 4
PREPARATION & COOKING TIME: 40 minutes
FREEZING: not recommended

PER SERVING: 376 calories, 10 g fat

Bulgar wheat (also known as cracked wheat) is so easy to cook. **Flavoured with spices, seeds and fruit**, it goes equally well with squashes, including pumpkins. Toast the pine nuts under the grill, turning them frequently, or over a low heat in a heavy-based pan. Serve with a side salad.

**1 butternut squash, weighing about 450 g (1 lb), peeled, halved and de-seeded and cut into 8 wedges**
**500 ml (18 fl oz) well flavoured vegetable stock, fresh if possible**
**175 g (6 oz) bulgar wheat**
**110 g (4 oz) ready-to-eat dried apricots, chopped**
**85 g (3 oz) ready-to-eat prunes, chopped**
**spray oil**
**1 onion, chopped**
**½–1 chilli, de-seeded and chopped finely**
**1 teaspoon ground cumin**
**1 teaspoon coriander seeds, crushed**
**40 g (1½ oz) pine nuts, toasted**
**2 tablespoons chopped fresh flat-leaf parsley or lemon balm**
**freshly ground black pepper**

1. Steam the squash slices until *just* tender, about 10 minutes depending on the age of the squash. Remove from the heat to a plate.
2. Pour the stock into a large pan and bring to the boil. Stir in the bulgar wheat, apricots and prunes. Cover and cook over a low heat for 20–25 minutes, until softened. If all the stock is absorbed before the cooking has finished, add a little more boiling stock or water; if the wheat is cooked before all the liquid is absorbed, evaporate the liquid over a high heat.
3. Preheat the grill to medium. Place the squash on a foil-lined grill pan and spray with oil, about 1 spray per slice.
4. Grill for 10–15 minutes until browned, turning once and spraying the other side. Once cooked, keep the squash warm.
5. Spray the base of a pan with oil. Add the onion and chilli and stir-fry for 3–4 minutes over a medium heat until cooked. Add the spices and cook for 30 seconds.
6. Stir the onion and spices, pine nuts and herbs into the wheat and fruits and serve with the squash.

# GRILLED BUTTERNUT SQUASH WITH SPICED BULGAR WHEAT

SERVES: 4
PREPARATION & COOKING TIME: 30 minutes
FREEZING: recommended

PER SERVING: 240 calories, 5 g fat

Though they **are traditionally a Christmas ingredient,** use chestnuts to make this sweet-flavoured casserole all through the wintertime.

# CHESTNUT CASSEROLE

**1 teaspoon oil**
**½ level teaspoon ground ginger**
**½ teaspoon grated nutmeg**
**a pinch of ground cloves**
**2 leeks, sliced**
**1 green pepper, de-seeded and sliced**
**1 red pepper, de-seeded and sliced**
**2 celery sticks, sliced**
**1 bay leaf**
**425 ml (¾ pint) vegetable stock**
**2 x 200 g packs cooked, whole peeled chestnuts**
**15 g (½ oz) flour**
**3 tablespoons skimmed milk**
**freshly ground black pepper**

1. Heat the oil in a large saucepan over a medium heat and fry the spices for 1 minute.
2. Add the vegetables and the bay leaf. Stir-fry for 1 minute, to mix the spices in well.
3. Pour the stock over the vegetables and bring to the boil. Simmer, covered, for 5 minutes.
4. If the chestnuts are packed closely, separate them. Add to the vegetables and simmer for a further 10 minutes.
5. Blend the flour to a smooth paste with the milk. Pour into the chestnut casserole, stirring briskly. Simmer for 1 minute. Season to taste with the pepper.

SERVES: 4
PREPARATION & COOKING TIME:
50 minutes + 25 minutes cooking
FREEZING: recommended

PER SERVING: 312 calories, 4 g fat

A **vegetarian version of the traditional recipe** that meat eaters will also enjoy. Serve with green vegetables and extra gravy.

# COTTAGE PIE

FOR THE TOPPING:

**1–2 parsnips, about 225 g (8 oz) prepared weight, cored and cut into large pieces**
**1–2 potatoes, about 225 g (8 oz) prepared weight, peeled and cut into pieces**
**freshly ground black pepper and freshly grated nutmeg**

FOR THE FILLING:

**½ tablespoon oil**
**1 onion, chopped**
**2 carrots, chopped finely**
**2 celery sticks, chopped into small pieces**
**225 g (8 oz) soya mince**
**300 ml (½ pint) vegetable stock**
**a bouquet garni or 1 teaspoon dried mixed herbs**
**freshly ground black pepper**

1. Prepare the topping. Bring a saucepan of water to the boil and add the parsnips and potatoes; the water should only just cover them. Cover with a lid, bring back to the boil and simmer for about 15 minutes until the vegetables are tender. Meanwhile, preheat the oven to Gas Mark 5/ electric oven 190°C/fan oven 170°C.
2. Prepare the filling. Gently heat the oil in a saucepan over a medium heat. Add the onion and fry for 3–4 minutes until softened. Add the carrot and celery and fry for a further 2 minutes.
3. Add the mince, stock and herbs to the fried vegetables, bring to the boil and simmer, covered, for 15 minutes or until the vegetables are tender.
4. When the topping vegetables are cooked, drain, reserving the cooking water. Mash the vegetables well. Add sufficient of the reserved cooking liquid to beat the mash to a creamy consistency. Season to taste with pepper and nutmeg.
5. If using a bouquet garni remove it from the mince mixture. Season the mince to taste with the pepper.
6. Spoon the mince mixture into an ovenproof pie dish. Pipe or spoon the topping over. If using a spoon even out with a knife and decorate with a fork.
7. Place the dish on a baking sheet and bake for 25 minutes, until golden and crisp on the top. If you like, use the remaining vegetable water to make vegetarian gravy to serve.

SERVES: 4
PREPARATION & COOKING TIME:
25 minutes + proving and resting + 25 minutes cooking
FREEZING: recommended

# PIZZA MARGHERITA

Pizza Margherita is one of the original pizzas and would usually be high in fat. This low fat version is **as delicious as the original.** Add a few olives if you like, but remember, they raise the fat content.

PER SERVING: 273 calories, 8 g fat

FOR THE DOUGH:
**175 g (6 oz) strong flour**
**¼ teaspoon salt**
**½ sachet dried yeast**
**½ tablespoon olive oil**
**90 ml (3 fl oz) warm water**

FOR THE SAUCE:
**375 g can of chopped tomatoes**
**1 shallot or very small onion, chopped finely**
**1 garlic clove, crushed**
**1 tablespoon tomato purée**
**1 teaspoon dried oregano**
**freshly ground black pepper**

FOR THE TOPPING:
**1 onion, sliced into rings**
**125 g (4½ oz) light mozzarella cheese**
**½ tablespoon olive oil**

1. Make the dough. Sieve the flour and salt. Stir in the yeast. Mix in the oil and then sufficient water to make a soft dough.
2. Knead the dough until it feels smooth and silky. Leave to prove, covered, in a warm place, for about 40 minutes, or until it has doubled in size.
3. Make the sauce. Drain the tomatoes well and reserve both the tomatoes and liquid. Cook the onion and garlic with the reserved tomato juice in a covered saucepan until softened. Add the remaining ingredients and simmer until a thick sauce is formed.
4. Cook the onion for the topping in sufficient water to cover it until it has softened. If there is still some liquid left, boil it hard to evaporate it. Slice the cheese about 5 mm (¼ inch) thick.
5. When the dough has proved, turn it on to a lightly floured surface. Knead for a minute and then roll into a circle about 23 cm (9 inches) across. Place the dough on a non-stick baking sheet or pizza dish and leave it to rest for 15 minutes. Meanwhile, preheat the oven to Gas Mark 6/electric oven 200°C/fan oven 180°C.
6. Brush the dough with the oil.
7. Spread the sauce over the oiled dough, place the onion rings over this and lastly add the slices of cheese.
8. Bake for 15–20 minutes, until the top is golden and the base cooked.

SERVES: 3
PREPARATION & COOKING TIME: 40 minutes
FREEZING: recommended

# MIXED MUSHROOM & RED WINE SAUCE

This **sophisticated sauce** can be served over a variety of foods to make them special. I like it poured over plain Quorn fillets but it can also be used over stir-fried tofu or steamed individual cauliflowers. If you are also cooking for meat-lovers, this is excellent over beef or turkey steaks.

PER SERVING: 129 calories, 1 g fat

**1 red onion, chopped finely**
**spray oil**
**110 g (4 oz) button mushrooms, wiped and sliced**
**55 g (2 oz) chestnut mushrooms, wiped and sliced**
**55 g (2 oz) oyster mushrooms, wiped and sliced**
**4 tablespoons brandy**
**200 ml (7 fl oz) red wine**
**2 teaspoons plain flour or cornflour**
**150 ml (5 fl oz) hot fresh vegetable stock**
**freshly ground black pepper**

1. Put the onion in a small heavy-based pan, cover and cook over a gentle heat until tender, this should take about 20 minutes.
2. Spray a non-stick frying pan with about 5 sprays of the oil. Add the mushrooms and stir-fry for 2 minutes over a medium heat.
3. Add the brandy to the mushrooms, bring to the boil and simmer without a lid for 1–2 minutes, until the liquid is reduced by half.
4. Pour in the red wine, add the onion and simmer for 5 minutes.
5. Mix the flour with a little cold water and blend to a smooth paste. Stir the stock into the paste.
6. Pour the blended stock into the pan of mushrooms and bring to the boil, stirring all the time.
7. Simmer gently for about 15 minutes, until the sauce has a syrupy consistency. Season to taste with black pepper.

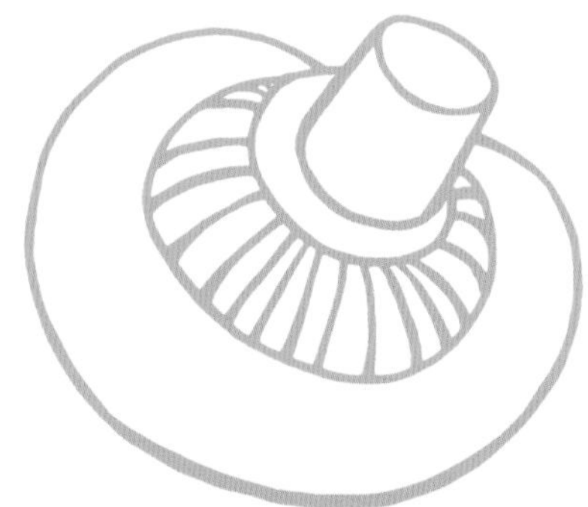

SERVES: 4
PREPARATION TIME: 15 minutes
FREEZING: not recommended

# COTTAGE CHEESE & HERB SALAD WITH STRAWBERRIES

This **light, refreshing salad** is ideal for summer lunches. Serve with crusty bread.

PER SERVING: 141 calories, 5 g fat

FOR THE DRESSING:
**2 tablespoons fresh orange juice**
**1 tablespoon lemon juice**
**1 tablespoon olive or rapeseed oil (optional)**
**freshly ground black pepper**

FOR THE COTTAGE CHEESE:
**400 g (14 oz) low fat cottage cheese**
**3–4 tablespoons chopped fresh herbs, e.g. basil, chives, dill, lemon balm, lemon or sweet thyme and/or salad burnet**
**freshly ground black pepper**

FOR THE SALAD:
**mixed salad leaves**
**200 g (7 oz) strawberries, halved or quartered or sliced if very large**
**20 chive stems, trimmed to 9 cm (3½ inches) long (optional)**

1. Make the dressing. Combine the juices, stir in the oil, if using, and season to taste with pepper.
2. Spoon the cottage cheese into a bowl and stir in the chosen herb(s) to taste. Judge how much and how many types to use depending on their strength of flavour. Season with pepper.
3. Pile the cottage cheese into the centre of four serving plates.
4. Scatter the salad leaves around the cheese.
5. Divide the strawberries between the plates, placing them amongst the salad leaves.
6. If using the chive stems, scatter these over the salad leaves.
7. Just before serving, stir the dressing. Serve it in a small jug or dish, separately from the salad.

# MEAT & FISH MAIN COURSE

White fish contains so little fat it is perfect for a low fat diet. Vary the fish given in the recipes: cod and haddock can be interchanged and any firm fish could replace the monkfish in Monkfish Kebabs with Couscous (page 39). Tuna is classed as an oily fish and contains the important omega-3 oil; even so, Fresh Tuna with Green Beans and Tomato (page 40) remains low in fat.

Red meat is where we need to be cautious, as it can contain a lot of saturated fat. However, if you serve it with plenty of vegetables you will need to eat less meat and so reduce your fat intake that way. White meat such as chicken has a much lower fat content and most of that is found under the skin; taking off the skin removes much of the fat.

So buy the fish and meat you enjoy, trim the fat where necessary, add all the flavouring ingredients and get cooking!

SERVES: 4
PREPARATION & COOKING TIME: 15 minutes + 12 minutes
FREEZING: not recommended

PER SERVING: 176 calories, 5 g fat

# BAKED COD IN A HERB & LEMON CRUST

A **crisp coating adds texture and flavour** to cod. Wholemeal breadcrumbs give a better flavour but white can be used. Use whichever herbs you have available: a mix of two or three is best. If you have to use dried herbs, reduce the quantity to 3 teaspoons. Serve with steamed new potatoes and green beans.

**4 x 125 g (4½ oz) pieces of thick cod fillet**
**55 g (2 oz) fresh wholemeal breadcrumbs**
**3 tablespoons chopped fresh herbs, e.g. parsley, thyme or lemon balm**
**1 small garlic clove, chopped finely**
**grated zest of 1 lemon**
**1 teaspoon lemon juice**
**1 tablespoon olive oil**
**freshly ground black pepper**

1. Preheat the oven to Gas Mark 6/electric oven200°C/fan oven 180°C.
2. Remove any bones from the cod and place the pieces on a baking sheet lined with non-stick paper. Season with black pepper.
3. Put the breadcrumbs, chopped herbs, garlic and lemon zest into a basin and mix well. Stir in the lemon juice and oil. Season with pepper.
4. Carefully spoon the breadcrumb mixture on top of the cod fillets, pressing it down well so that it stays in place.
5. Bake for about 12 minutes, until the top is golden and the fish cooked. Serve immediately.

SERVES: 1
PREPARATION & COOKING TIME: 25 minutes
FREEZING: not recommended

PER SERVING: 375 calories, 3 g fat

# TUNA PASTA SALAD

A **quick and tasty** dish for when you are on your own at lunchtime; it can easily be doubled to serve two. Vary the vegetables according to what you have available; the only limit is your imagination! If you enjoy garlic you could crush a small clove and stir it into the dressing. Other herbs will work as well as basil: try parsley, oregano or dill. Serve with crusty bread for a more substantial meal.

FOR THE SALAD:
**55 g (2 oz) dried pasta, e.g. spirals or shells**
**55 g (2 oz) frozen sweetcorn kernels**
**1 small leek, sliced**
**1 celery stick, sliced**
**3 cherry tomatoes, halved**
**75 g can of tuna in water, drained well and broken into chunks**

FOR THE DRESSING:
**1 tablespoon low fat natural yogurt**
**½ teaspoon lemon juice or balsamic vinegar**
**½ tablespoon chopped fresh basil or ½ teaspoon dried basil**
**freshly ground black pepper**

1. Cook the pasta according to the packet instructions. Drain and rinse straight away under cold running water until the pasta is cold. Leave to drain.
2. Steam the sweetcorn and leek until just cooked, 4–5 minutes. As soon as they are cooked, tip into a strainer and cool under running cold water; or plunge them into iced water. When the vegetables are cold, drain them well.
3. Prepare the dressing: combine the yogurt, lemon juice or vinegar and basil and season to taste with pepper.
4. Ensure the pasta and cooked vegetables are as dry as possible.
5. Combine all the ingredients for the salad and stir in the dressing. If not to be eaten immediately, store in the refrigerator.

SERVES: 4
PREPARATION & COOKING TIME:
2 hours marinating + 30 minutes
COOKING TIME: 15 minutes
FREEZING: not recommended

# MONKFISH KEBABS WITH COUSCOUS

The **firmness** of monkfish flesh makes it **ideal for kebabs.** They can, of course, be barbecued instead of grilled. Choose herbs which complement each other as well as the fish. A side salad makes a good accompaniment.

PER SERVING: 218 calories, 1 g fat

**3 tablespoons reduced-salt soy sauce**
**3 tablespoons lemon juice**
**2 garlic cloves, crushed**
**225 g (8 oz) couscous**
**300 ml (½ pint) boiling vegetable stock**
**2 tablespoons mixed chopped fresh herbs, e.g. thyme, lemon balm, chives, parsley and/or oregano**
**freshly ground black pepper**

FOR THE KEBABS:
**400 g (14 oz) monkfish, cut into 4 cm (1 ½ -inch) pieces**
**2 courgettes, cut into 1 cm (½ -inch) pieces**
**4 shallots, halved**
**4 cherry tomatoes**

1. Mix together the soy sauce, lemon juice and garlic. Season with pepper.
2. Place the fish pieces in a shallow dish and pour the marinade over them. Cover and leave for 2 hours in a refrigerator.
3. Thread the monkfish and vegetables on to skewers, alternating the ingredients.
4. Place the kebabs on a baking sheet and grill them under a medium heat for 15 minutes, or until they are cooked.
5. Spoon the couscous into a basin and pour the boiling stock over. Cover and leave to stand for 5 minutes. Stir in the herbs and season with pepper.
6. Fork the couscous to make it fluffy, spoon it on to serving plates and place the kebabs on top.

# FRESH TUNA WITH GREEN BEANS & TOMATO

SERVES: 2
PREPARATION & COOKING TIME: 40 minutes
FREEZING: not recommended

PER SERVING: 224 calories, 5 g fat

Fresh tuna is one of the oily fish that **we should be eating at least once a week.** If you prefer, cook the tuna steaks on a ridged griddle or in an oiled frying pan for 2–3 minutes on each side. This will only very slightly increase the fat content and the tuna will be firmer, drier and have more colour. Serve with boiled new potatoes in their skins.

**½ teaspoon oil**
**1 small onion, chopped finely**
**2 tuna fish steaks, each about 1.5 cm (⅝ inch) thick**
**2 tablespoons white wine or 1 tablespoon water mixed with 1 tablespoon fresh lime juice**
**200 g (7 oz) green beans, left whole if small (about 10 cm/4 inches long)**
**6 cherry tomatoes**
**½ tablespoon chopped fresh basil or ½ teaspoon dried basil**
**freshly ground black pepper**

1. Heat the oil in a heavy-based small saucepan. Add the onion, cover and cook over a very low heat for 10–15 minutes, until the onion is softened and golden in colour.
2. Preheat the oven to Gas Mark 6/electric oven 200°C/fan oven 180°C and prepare a steamer for the beans.
3. Cover a baking sheet with foil and place the tuna steaks in the centre of this. Season well with black pepper and then lift the foil at the edges to form a 'wall'. Pour the wine or water over the fish and then fold the foil to make a loose parcel. Bake for 15 minutes, or until the steaks are tender.
4. Meanwhile, steam the beans until tender, about 8–10 minutes.
5. When the onion is ready, add the cherry tomatoes and cook with the lid on until the skins have split and the tomatoes are hot, 4–5 minutes. If using dried basil, add it now.
6. Divide the beans between two plates, spoon the tomato mixture over them and sprinkle with the fresh basil, if using. Place a tuna steak on top or by the side of each portion of vegetables.

SERVES: 5
PREPARATION & COOKING TIME:
50 minutes + 30 minutes cooking
FREEZING: recommended

PER SERVING: 210 calories, 3 g fat

The **delicious flavour of smoked haddock** combines well with the mushrooms and ricotta cheese to give a low fat lasagne. Smoked cod works just as well. Serve with a green salad.

FOR THE SAUCE:
**600 ml (1 pint) skimmed milk**
**1 onion, halved**
**2 cloves (optional)**
**1 bay leaf**
**6 level tablespoons cornflour**
**300 ml (½ pint) fish stock (from cooking the fish)**
**15 g (½ oz) low fat spread**
**freshly grated nutmeg and freshly ground black pepper**

FOR THE FILLING:
**400 g (14 oz) undyed smoked haddock fillet, skinned**
**200 g (7 oz) mushrooms, wiped and chopped**
**3 tablespoons ricotta cheese**
**2 tablespoons chopped fresh chives**
**6 sheets no-egg dried lasagne**

1. Measure 90 ml (3 fl oz) of the milk into a basin. Pour the remaining milk into a saucepan, add the onion halves, cloves and bay leaf and bring to the boil. When the milk is at boiling point, remove it from the heat, cover with a lid and leave the flavourings to infuse.
2. Place the smoked haddock in a wide, shallow pan, cover with cold water and bring to the boil. As soon as boiling point is reached, discard the water; this will remove some of the salt. Cover again with cold water and bring to the boil.
3. Once boiling point is reached again, remove from the heat and cover with a lid. Leave for 5 minutes, then test to see if the fish is cooked. If it is, drain off the fish stock and reserve (otherwise reheat the water and leave for another minute or two). It is important for the flavour and texture that the fish is only *just* cooked.
4. Allow the fish to cool for a few minutes, then flake it, removing any bones you notice. Mix with the mushrooms, ricotta cheese and chives. Season with the pepper.
5. Measure the reserved stock. If necessary make it up to the required 300 ml (½ pint) with water.
6. Blend the cornflour with the reserved cold milk to make a smooth paste.
7. Remove the flavouring ingredients from the infused milk and add the fish stock to it. Heat to boiling point. Pour the boiling liquid over the cornflour paste, stirring constantly to mix well.
8. Return the sauce to the pan, add the low fat spread and bring to the boil. Simmer gently for 1 minute, stirring all the time. Season with the nutmeg and pepper. The sauce will be thin because the lasagne sheets need to absorb some of the liquid.
9. Preheat the oven to Gas mark 4/electric oven 180°C/fan oven 160°C.
10. Pour one-third of the sauce into the base of a shallow ovenproof dish. Place half the lasagne sheets over this, not allowing them to overlap. Spoon half the fish mixture over the lasagne sheets. Repeat the layers, finishing with the sauce.
11. Place the dish on a baking sheet in the oven and bake for 30 minutes, until the lasagne is hot and bubbling.

# SMOKED HADDOCK LASAGNE

# SWEET VEGETABLE & BEEF CASSEROLE

SERVES: 4
PREPARATION & COOKING TIME: 30 minutes + about 2 ½ hours cooking
FREEZING: recommended

PER SERVING: 310 calories, 8 g fat

In a traditional beef casserole, the meat is often fried in oil with some of the vegetables to develop a sweeter flavour. In this recipe, however, the **onion is caramelised and several sweet vegetables are included** to create a similar effect. Serve with either a plain baked potato or Herby Dumplings (page 50).

**1 onion, sliced**
**1–2 carrots, weighing about 200 g (7 oz), chopped**
**1–2 leeks, weighing about 200 g (7 oz), chopped**
**1–2 parsnips, weighing about 200 g (7 oz), chopped**
**1 sweet potato, peeled and chopped**
**225 ml (8 fl oz) beef stock**
**225 ml (8 fl oz) beer, ale or lager**
**450 g (1 lb) lean casserole beef pieces, trimmed of any remaining fat**
**a bouquet garni**
**2 level tablespoons cornflour**
**freshly ground black pepper**

1. Put the onion slices in a small, heavy-based pan, cover with the lid and place over a low heat. Leave to become golden brown and slightly sticky. Check after 15 minutes to ensure the onion is beginning to brown; if not, raise the heat a little. When the onion is cooked and coloured, remove from the heat (this should take about 30 minutes in total).
2. Preheat the oven to Gas Mark 3/electric oven170°C/fan oven 150°C.
3. Place all the other vegetables, in a flameproof casserole (one that can go on the hob as well as in the oven); or use a heavy-based frying pan. Pour on the stock and beer. Cover and bring to the boil. Stir well.
4. Add the meat and bouquet garni to the vegetables and season with pepper. Stir in the caramelised onion. If you have used a frying pan, spoon the meat and vegetable mixture into a casserole dish and cover with the lid. Place on a baking sheet and then transfer to the oven. Cook for 1 ¼–1 ½ hours, or until the meat and vegetables are *just* tender. Mix the cornflour to a smooth paste with a little cold water.
5. Remove the casserole from the oven. Pour the cornflour paste over and stir, taking care not to break the vegetables. Replace the lid and return the casserole to the oven for another 20 minutes. Remove the bouquet garni and serve.

COOK'S TIP: Don't be tempted to cook the casserole for longer in step 3, because really lean cuts of meat seem to toughen very quickly, even in a casserole. They don't seem to break down as do the traditional casserole cuts.

# TURKEY STIR-FRY WITH ORANGE & REDCURRANT SAUCE

SERVES: 2
PREPARATION & COOKING TIME: 35 minutes
FREEZING: not recommended

PER SERVING: 270 calories, 4 g fat

Turkey is an **ideal choice for low fat eating**. The vegetables in this stir-fry remain very crisp; if you prefer them softer add them to the wok at the same time or just after the turkey. Cranberries can be used in place of the redcurrants; these would not need sieving and some could be reserved to add whole to the stir-fry at the same time as the sauce is added.

Serve this light dish with salad and either Naan Breads (page 56), crusty bread or rice.

FOR THE SAUCE:
**150 g (5½ oz) fresh or frozen redcurrants**
**1 teaspoon grated orange zest**
**juice of 1 orange**
**about 1 tablespoon light soft brown sugar**
**lemon juice, to taste (optional)**

FOR THE STIR-FRY:
**½ sweet potato, peeled**
**1 courgette, trimmed**
**200 g (7 oz) turkey stir-fry pieces**
**½ teaspoon oil**

1 Make the sauce first. Put the redcurrants, orange zest and juice in a pan and bring to the boil. Simmer for 7–8 minutes or until the currants are tender. Stir in the sugar and stir until it has dissolved.
2 Press the sauce through a sieve to remove the seeds. It should be slightly syrupy. If it is not, boil again for 1 or 2 minutes to reduce it. Taste for sweetness. If necessary, adjust with more sugar or a little lemon juice.
3 Cut the sweet potato into four lengthways and then cut each piece into thin slivers. Cut the courgette into four lengthways and then cut each piece into 3 mm (⅛ **-inch**) slices, or thinner. If necessary, cut the stir-fry turkey into evenly sized pieces.
4 Heat the oil in a wok or large frying pan. Add the turkey and stir-fry for 4–5 minutes, until it is just cooked and the juices run clear when pierced and pressed. Add the vegetables and stir-fry for 2 minutes.
6 Spoon in the sauce and stir-fry for 1 minute to heat through. Serve immediately.

SERVES: 6
PREPARATION & COOKING TIME:
35 minutes + 1¼ hours cooking
FREEZING: recommended

# PORK & PLUM CASSEROLE

Pork and plums are **perfect partners**. Best cooked in the late summer, this casserole can be made all year round, but do make sure the plums are ripe. If you prefer, the quantity of wine can be halved and stock used in its place. Serve with mashed potatoes and your choice of green vegetable.

PER SERVING: 219 calories, 4 g fat

**1 teaspoon oil**
**1½ teaspoons five-spice powder**
**1 red onion, sliced**
**1 cooking onion, sliced**
**2 garlic cloves, sliced**
**3 celery sticks, sliced**
**2 teaspoons dried basil**
**675 g (1½ lb) lean pork, cubed**
**300 ml (½ pint) red wine**
**450 g (1 lb) ripe red plums, quartered and stoned**
**1 tablespoon cornflour**
**freshly ground black pepper**
**chopped fresh parsley, to garnish (optional)**

1. Preheat the oven to Gas Mark 3/electric oven 170°C/fan oven 150°C.
2. Heat the oil in a frying pan. Add the five-spice powder and cook over a gentle heat for 30 seconds.
3. Add the onions and garlic and stir-fry for 2 minutes. Add the celery and stir-fry for 1 minute.
4. Sprinkle on the basil and stir in the pork and wine, with three-quarters of the plums. Bring to the boil and immediately tip into a casserole dish. Cover, place on a baking sheet and cook at for about 1¼ hours, or until the pork is just tender.
5. Blend the cornflour to a smooth paste with a little cold water. Stir into the casserole, mixing it through all the liquid. Place the remaining plums on top and return to the oven for 15 minutes, or until the plums have heated through.
6. If you like, garnish with chopped fresh parsley.

SERVES: 4
PREPARATION & COOKING TIME: 30 minutes
FREEZING: not recommended

# CHICKEN WITH MANGO SAUCE

This **sweet, golden sauce** marries beautifully with the **delicate flavour** of the chicken. Adding the zest gives the sauce more of a tang. One large, skinless chicken breast fillet per person can be used, if preferred, increasing the cooking time accordingly. This dish can be served either hot or cold, with a side salad and couscous or rice.

PER SERVING: 212 calories, 5 g fat

**12 mini chicken breast fillets**
**6 tablespoons white wine**
**1 small ripe mango**
**2 tablespoons lemon or lime juice**
**1–2 teaspoons lemon or lime zest (optional)**
**freshly ground pepper (white if available)**
**2 tablespoons chopped fresh parsley or thyme, to garnish**

1. Preheat the oven to Gas Mark 4/electric oven 180°C/fan oven 160°C.
2. Place the chicken fillets in a dish in a single layer and pour the wine over them. Cover closely with foil and bake for 15 minutes, or until cooked. To test the fillets, pierce one of the centre ones with a sharp, pointed knife; the juices will be clear when cooked. If any sign of pinkness remains, cook for a little longer.
3. Meanwhile, prepare the sauce. Peel the mango and remove the stone. Chop the flesh and place in a food processor, with the fruit juice and zest (if using). Blend until smooth. When the chicken is cooked, drain off the juices and add these to the sauce. Blend briefly. Season to taste with pepper. If serving hot, reheat the sauce.
4. Serve three fillets on each plate, with the sauce poured by the side. Any remaining sauce can be served separately, in a small jug.
5. Scatter the parsley or thyme over the chicken or carefully spoon a little between each fillet.
6. If serving cold, store both chicken and sauce in a refrigerator, removing them 30 minutes before serving.

SERVES: 3
PREPARATION & COOKING TIME: 30 minutes
FREEZING: not recommended

# STIR-FRY LAMB FILLET ON A BED OF AUBERGINE

Cooked quickly, the **lamb retains its full sweet flavour**. The aubergine slices can be grilled if you prefer a firmer texture, following the method for Baby Aubergine & Courgette Platter (page 22). The slices will cook in about 3 minutes each side.

Serve with a green salad and crusty bread.

PER SERVING: 129 calories, 3 g fat

**1 aubergine, cut into 5 mm (¼ inch) slices**
**lemon juice**
**200 g lean lamb fillet, sliced into thin strips about 9 cm (3½ inches) long, excess fat removed**
**8 spring onions, cut into 5 mm (¼ inch) pieces**
**2–3 garlic cloves, chopped finely**
**16 cherry tomatoes, halved**
**2 tablespoons chopped fresh herbs, e.g. rosemary, thyme and/or parsley,**
**freshly ground black pepper**

1. Brush the aubergine slices with lemon juice to prevent discoloration. Prepare a steamer for the aubergine slices. Bring the water to the boil.
2. Meanwhile, spoon 2 tablespoons of water into the base of a wok or large frying pan. Bring to the boil and add the lamb, spring onions and garlic. 'Stir-fry' for 2 minutes.
3. When the steamer is ready, place the aubergine slices in it and cook until tender, about 3 minutes.
4. Add the tomatoes and herbs to the lamb and 'stir-fry' for 1–2 minutes or until the lamb is cooked and the vegetables hot. Season with pepper to taste.
5. Arrange the aubergine slices on individual serving plates and spoon the stir-fry on top. Serve immediately.

So often we have a great idea for the main part of a meal, but then the question is what to serve with it? Here are lots of ideas for you, from dumplings and breads to salads and vegetables. Mix and match them with different dishes to create varying menus. Change the herbs or

# ACCOMPANIMENTS

other flavours to complement the taste of the main dish.

Gone is the era of soggy or greasy vegetables, heavily dressed salads or dumplings full of saturated fat; now is the time to think fresh and light.

SERVES: 4
PREPARATION & COOKING TIME: 10 minutes + 20 minutes
FREEZING: recommended

# HERBY DUMPLINGS

Serve these **little dumplings** with any casserole or stew – they go beautifully with Sweet Vegetable & Beef Casserole (page 43).

PER SERVING: 144 calories, 5 g fat

**110 g (4 oz) self-raising flour**
**25 g (1 oz) soft spread (see page 10)**
**1 tablespoon mixed chopped fresh herbs or 1 teaspoon dried mixed herbs**
**4–6 tablespoons natural low fat yogurt**

1. Spoon the flour into a basin and rub in the spread. Stir in the herbs.
2. Mix in sufficient yogurt to make a soft but not sticky dough.
3. Handling lightly, divide the dough into eight pieces and roll into balls.
4. Place the dumplings on top of the casserole or stew, cover and cook for about 20 minutes, until risen and cooked.

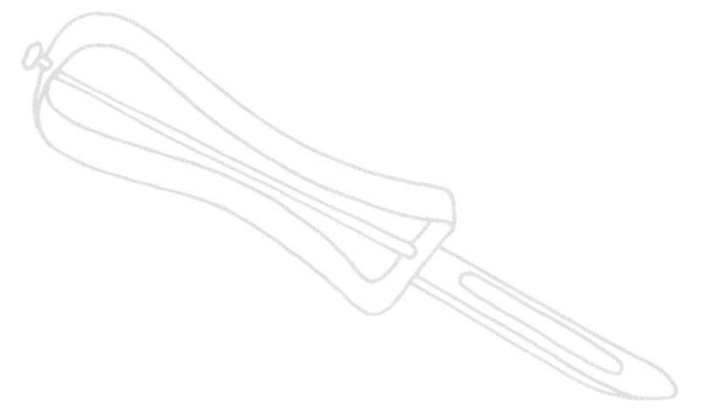

SERVES: 10–12
PREPARATION & COOKING TIME: 25 minutes + proving + 45 minutes
FREEZING: recommended

# POTATO BREAD

Based on a **traditional recipe**, the addition of herbs makes this **lovely moist bread** even more flavoursome. Choose herbs to complement the dish you are serving with the bread – potato bread goes well with soups, stews and hotpots and is at its most delicious served warm.

PER SERVING: 135 calories, 1 g fat

**225 g (8 oz) strong white flour**
**225 g (8 oz) strong wholemeal flour**
**1 sachet easy-blend dried yeast**
**1 teaspoon salt**
**1 tablespoon dried mixed herbs or 3 tablespoons mixed chopped fresh herbs**
**110 g (4 oz) warm cooked potato, mashed without added fat**
**300 ml (½ pint) warm mixed skimmed milk and water**

1. Mix together the flours, yeast and salt. Stir in the herbs. Rub in the warm mashed potato with your fingers and thumbs. Add enough of the milk and water to make a soft dough.
2. Turn on to a lightly floured work surface and knead until the dough feels smooth and silky. Cover and leave to prove in a warm place until doubled in size.
3. Knock back the dough with your fist, to deflate it. Then knead lightly, form into a loaf shape and place in a greased 1 kg (2 lb) loaf tin. Cover and leave to prove in a warm place, until the dough has risen to the top of the tin.
4. Preheat the oven to Gas Mark 7/electric oven 220°C/fan oven 200°C.
5. Bake the bread for about 45 minutes, until the base sounds hollow when tapped. If the top starts to brown early on in the baking, cover it with foil to prevent it from becoming too brown. Cool on a wire rack.

SERVES: 2
PREPARATION & COOKING TIME: 15 minutes
FREEZING: not recommended

# WARM MUSHROOM SALAD WITH LEMON

Warm salads are **tempting all year round**. This one complements poultry, beef and vegetarian options such as Quorn dishes.

PER SERVING: 32 calories, 1 g fat

**250 g (9 oz) chestnut mushrooms, wiped**
**150 g (5 ½ oz) button mushrooms, wiped**
**2 garlic cloves, chopped finely**
**grated zest of ½ lemon**
**2 tablespoons lemon juice**
**1 tablespoon chopped fresh parsley**
**freshly ground black pepper**

TO SERVE:
**a few lettuce leaves, not bitter**
**2 tablespoons rocket leaves**

1. Halve or quarter the chestnut mushrooms, depending on size. Leave the button mushrooms whole or halve if they are large.
2. Arrange the lettuce and rocket leaves on serving plates
3. Put the mushrooms, garlic, lemon zest and juice into a wok or large frying pan and 'stir-fry' for 3–4 minutes, until hot. Juice will start to run from the mushrooms so it will not burn. Add the parsley and stir-fry for 30 seconds. Season to taste with pepper.
4. Remove from the wok, using a slotted spoon, and spoon on to the lettuce and rocket leaves.
5. Evaporate the remaining juices until there are only 1–2 teaspoons left and drizzle over the salad. Serve immediately.

MAKES: 6
PREPARATION & COOKING TIME: 20 minutes
COOKING TIME: 15 minutes
FREEZING: recommended

# WATERCRESS SCONES

These **deliciously light scones are wonderful served with soup**, when any spread is really unnecessary. They could also be served for a snack, spread thinly with low fat cottage cheese or Quark. Adding a little orange zest to either of these spreads adds an extra tang to the flavour.

PER SERVING: 202 calories, 7 g fat

**225 g (8 oz) self-raising flour**
**55 g (2 oz) soft spread (see page 10)**
**85 g bag of watercress, tough stalks removed, leaves chopped finely**
**150 ml (5 fl oz) natural yogurt**
**skimmed milk, to glaze**

1. Preheat the oven to Gas Mark 7/electric oven 220°C/fan oven 200°C. Lightly grease a baking sheet.
2. Spoon the flour into a mixing bowl and rub in the spread. Stir the watercress into the rubbed in mixture and then carefully mix in the yogurt. Draw the mixture together gently and turn on to a lightly floured surface.
3. Knead the dough lightly and form it into a round. Pat out with the heel of your hand to about 2 cm (¾ inch) thick. Cut the round into six triangles with a sharp knife, being careful not to drag the knife across the dough.
4. Place the triangles on the greased baking sheet and brush with milk.
5. Place in the oven and bake for 15–20 minutes, until the base sounds hollow when tapped. Cool on a wire rack.

SERVES: 4
PREPARATION TIME: 15 minutes
FREEZING: not recommended

# BEETROOT & ORANGE SALAD

Make this salad when **oranges** are at their **best, in the winter time.** Serve alongside a green salad, including watercress or rocket for their peppery flavour to contrast with the sweetness of beetroot and orange.

PER SERVING: 57 calories, 1 g fat

**2 beetroots,**
**2 oranges**
**1 tablespoon white wine or wine vinegar**
**freshly ground black pepper**
**1 teaspoon toasted sesame seeds (optional)**

1. Put the beetroots into a pan of water. Bring to the boil and simmer for 20–25 minutes until tender. Drain and leave to cool. Wearing a pair of rubber gloves, gently rub the beetroot until the skins peel off.Slice the beetroots to about 3 mm (1/8 inch) thick.
2. Peel and segment the oranges, removing all the pips and as much pith as possible. Retain any juice that runs from the oranges.
3. Mix together the orange juice and the wine or vinegar to make a dressing. Season with pepper.
4. Arrange the beetroot slices and orange segments on a plate. Drizzle the dressing over the salad. If liked, sprinkle with the sesame seeds.

SERVES: 8
PREPARATION TIME: 20 minutes
FREEZING: not recommended

# MIXED MELON & TOMATO SALAD WITH MINT

This **combination is so refreshing**; serve it in the heat of summer as part of a mixed buffet or with poultry, ham or a soft cheese.

PER SERVING: 38 calories, 0 g fat

**1/2 Piel de Sapo or honeydew melon, peeled and de-seeded**
**1 Charentais or cantaloupe melon, peeled and de-seeded**
**200 g (7 oz) cherry tomatoes**
**2 tablespoons chopped fresh apple mint**
**freshly ground black pepper**

FOR THE DRESSING:
**3 tablespoons fresh orange juice**
**1–3 teaspoons balsamic vinegar**

1. Prepare the salad. Cut the flesh from both melons into 1 cm (1/2 -inch) cubes, place in a bowl and stir in the cherry tomatoes and mint. Season with pepper. Cover and chill.
2. Prepare the dressing. Stir together the juice and vinegar to taste and season with pepper. Pour into a small non-metallic jug or bowl. Cover and chill.
3. Just before serving stir the dressing into the salad, or serve it separately.

SERVES: 4
PREPARATION & COOKING TIME: 25 minutes
FREEZING: not recommended

# BROCCOLI & CAULIFLOWER FLORETS IN A RED PEPPER SAUCE

A sauce always adds interest to vegetables but so often is high in fat. The only fat in this is in the **small sprinkling of toasted almonds**. Don't be tempted to leave them out, though, as they really enhance the flavour. The red pepper sauce can also be used over grilled chicken fillets or cooked Quorn fillets, or as an alternative to the smoked haddock mixture in Baby Aubergine & Courgette Platter (page 22).

PER SERVING: 69 calories, 2 g fat

FOR THE SAUCE:
**1 red pepper, de-seeded and halved lengthways**
**1 onion, sliced**
**1–2 garlic cloves, chopped (optional)**
**2 tablespoons tomato purée**
**2 tablespoons lemon juice**
**freshly ground black pepper**

TO SERVE:
**200 g (7 oz) broccoli, cut into evenly sized florets**
**200 g (7 oz) cauliflower, cut into evenly sized florets**
**1 tablespoon flaked almonds, toasted**

1. Preheat the grill to hot. Place the pepper halves on foil on a grill pan and grill until blackened all over. It may be necessary to turn the halves to complete the colouring. When the skin has blackened, remove from the grill pan and place in a polythene bag. Leave until cool.
2. Meanwhile, put the onion slices into a small pan, barely cover with boiling water and simmer with the lid on the pan for 5 minutes.
3. Add the garlic (if using), the tomato purée and lemon juice to the onion and remaining water.
4. Remove the skins from the peppers and chop the flesh. Add to the onion mixture. Simmer for 10 minutes with the lid on. Cool.
5. Pour the sauce into a blender and process briefly until a coarse texture is achieved.
6. Steam the broccoli and cauliflower for 10 minutes or until tender – this will depend upon the size of the florets.
7. Reheat the sauce and season to taste with black pepper.
8. Spoon the vegetables on to a shallow serving dish and pour the sauce over. Scatter the almonds on top. Serve immediately.

SERVES: 4
PREPARATION & COOKING TIME:
10 minutes + 40 minutes cooking
FREEZING: not recommended

# VEGETABLE 'CHIPS'

These colourful 'chips' are **bursting with a variety of flavours**. With a softer texture than traditional chips, they make a good accompaniment to meat, fish and vegetarian dishes. 'Roast' vegetables can be cooked in the same way by cutting them into pieces and boiling or steaming them until they are partly cooked, draining well, then putting into the tin and spraying with oil.

PER SERVING: 139 calories, 3 g fat

**1–2 carrots, about 175 g (6 oz)**
**1 potato, about 175 g (6 oz), peeled**
**1 sweet potato, weighing about 175 g (6 oz), peeled**
**110 g (4 oz) swede**
**1 parsnip, about 175 g (6 oz), cored if woody**
**about 16 sprays of spray oil**

1. Preheat the oven to Gas Mark 6/electric oven 200°C/fan oven 180°C.
2. If the carrot is old and large start with this. Cut it into chip-sized pieces, place it in a pan with sufficient boiling water to cover it and boil for 3–4 minutes, until half cooked. Drain well and then dry on kitchen paper.
3. Cut all the other vegetables into chip-sized pieces, keeping them as evenly sized as possible. The trimmings can be used in soup.
4. Spray the base of a large roasting tin with oil. About 6 sprays will be needed, depending on the size of the tin. Place the vegetable 'chips' in the tin in a single layer. Spray the 'chips' with oil.
5. Bake for about 40 minutes, until golden brown and tender. Serve immediately.

SERVES: 4
PREPARATION & COOKING TIME:
15 minutes + 20 minutes cooking
FREEZING: recommended

# CELERIAC & POTATO PURÉE

Adding celeriac to potato adds **another dimension to the traditional mash**, whilst the chives brighten the appearance. Use this dish in place of plain mashed potato.

PER SERVING: 124 calories, 1 g fat

**500 g (1 lb 2 oz) celeriac, peeled and cut into chunks**
**500 g (1 lb 2 oz) potato, peeled and cut into chunks**
**1 tablespoon snipped fresh chives**
**1 tablespoon natural low fat yogurt, if necessary**
**freshly ground black pepper**

1. Bring a saucepan of water to the boil and add the celeriac and potato chunks. Cover and bring back to the boil. Cook for 15–20 minutes, until the vegetables are tender.
2. Drain the vegetables very well and then mash them. If the mixture is not really smooth, push it through a sieve.
3. Beat the chives into the purée. If the mixture is fairly dry, add a tablespoon of natural yogurt. Season to taste with pepper.

# NAAN BREADS

MAKES: 6 naans
PREPARATION & COOKING TIME:
30 minutes + 40 minutes proving
FREEZING: recommended

PER SERVING: 282 calories, 3 g fat

Naan bread can have quite a lot of saturated fat in it but this recipe keeps the basic **characteristics of naan** whilst **reducing the fat**. The seeds add interest; just make sure the flavour you choose complements the dish with which you are serving it.

**450 g (1 lb) strong white flour**
**½ teaspoon salt**
**1 sachet easy-blend dried yeast**
**2 teaspoons black onion seeds or cumin seeds or 1 teaspoon fennel seeds (all optional)**
**25 g (1 oz) low fat spread**
**300 ml (½ pint) skimmed milk, warmed**

1. Spoon the flour into a mixing bowl and add the salt and yeast. Sprinkle in the seeds (if using) and mix well.
2. Rub in the fat and then pour in most of the warmed milk. Work the milk into the dry mixture, adding the remaining liquid if needed, until a soft dough is formed.
3. Knead until the dough feels silky, 5–10 minutes. Place in a clean bowl, cover and leave to prove in a warm place until the dough has doubled in size – about 40 minutes.
4. When the dough has proved, knock it back with your fist, to deflate it; then knead for about 30 seconds.
5. Divide into six pieces. Flatten and roll each piece to about 5 mm (¼ inch) thick, pulling it into the traditional 'tear drop' shape. Prick the naan breads with a fork.
6. Heat the grill to medium. Lightly grease and warm a baking sheet.
7. Place as many naan breads on the baking sheet as will fit without touching. Grill the naan for 2–3 minutes until golden and then turn them over and grill the other side. It is important not to let them burn – lower the grill heat if necessary. Repeat with the other breads, keeping the first ones warm by wrapping them in foil. Serve warm.

Low fat desserts can be just as tempting as those laden with fat (and therefore calories). Often they are more refreshing to eat and they leave you without that 'I've eaten too much' feeling. Lower-fat versions of some of the traditional desserts loved by so many are included here; so everything from Steamed

# DESSERTS

Chocolate & Pear Pudding (page 60) to Strawberry Pavlova (page 64) can remain on the menu. I have also enjoyed experimenting with new recipes and hope that you will also feel inspired to try those less familiar to you. Just add the ingredients to your shopping list, then you'll be ready to start!

SERVES: 4
PREPARATION & COOKING TIME: 15 minutes + 1 hour cooking
FREEZING: recommended

# STEAMED CHOCOLATE & PEAR PUDDING

Serve this warming winter pudding with Chocolate Sauce (right) – no need to feel guilty, it really is low in fat!

PER SERVING: 284 calories, 8 g fat

**1 pear, weighing about 175 g (6 oz)**
**1 teaspoon lemon juice**
**55 g (2 oz) low fat spread**
**55 g (2 oz) light soft brown sugar**
**1 egg, beaten**
**100 g (3½ oz) self-raising flour**
**½ teaspoon baking powder**
**25 g (1 oz) cocoa powder**
**55 g (2 oz) golden syrup, warmed**

1. Peel, core and dice the pear and toss in the lemon juice to prevent it from browning.
2. Cream together the low fat spread and sugar and then beat in the egg.
3. Sieve together the flour, baking powder and cocoa. Fold these into the creamed mixture.
4. Fold in the golden syrup and the diced pear.
5. Spoon the mixture into a greased 600 ml (1 pint) pudding basin or four individual basins and cover either with a greased lid or with a double thickness of greaseproof paper, well secured.
6. Place in a steamer and steam for 45 minutes for the individual puddings, 1 hour for the large pudding, or until a skewer inserted into the centre comes out clean.

SERVES: 4
PREPARATION & COOKING TIME: 10 minutes
FREEZING: not recommended

# CHOCOLATE SAUCE

This is a delicious chocolate sauce to serve with Steamed Chocolate & Pear Pudding (left); you could also try it with stewed pears or poured over sliced banana. Skimmed milk is lower in fat, but using semi-skimmed makes the sauce creamier.

PER SERVING: 116 calories, 1 g fat

**3 tablespoons cornflour**
**1½ tablespoons cocoa powder**
**1½ tablespoons sugar, or to taste**
**425 ml (¾ pint) skimmed or semi-skimmed milk**

1. Mix the cornflour, cocoa and sugar with a little of the measured milk to form a smooth paste.
2. Heat the remaining milk in a saucepan to just below boiling point.
3. Pour the hot milk on to the blended mixture, stirring well. Ensure the liquid is well mixed.
4. Return the mixture to the saucepan and bring to the boil, stirring constantly.
5. Reduce the heat and allow the sauce to simmer for 20–30 seconds, still stirring. Check for sweetness, adding more sugar if necessary.
6. Pour into a serving jug or dish and serve immediately.

SERVES: 4
PREPARATION TIME: 15 minutes
FREEZING: recommended

# RASPBERRY COULIS

This **richly flavoured** coulis will make fresh fruit into a dessert; try it over bananas or sliced ripe pears. You could also stir fresh strawberries into it.

PER SERVING: 39 calories, 0 g fat

**225 g (8 oz) fresh or thawed frozen raspberries**
**about 25 g (1 oz) icing sugar, sifted**

1 Liquidise the raspberries if fresh ones are used.
2 Push the fresh purée or the thawed, frozen raspberries through a sieve, to remove the pips.
3 Add icing sugar to taste. Stir well. Serve chilled or at room temperature.

SERVES: 5
PREPARATION TIME: 20 minutes + chilling
FREEZING: not recommended

# SALAD OF THE SUN

Prepare this **exotic fruit salad** up to a day in advance to allow the **flavours to blend**. Leave adding the banana until 2 hours before serving so that it does not discolour.

PER SERVING: 91 calories, 0 g fat

**2 oranges**
**2 passion-fruit**
**1 peach**
**1 nectarine**
**1 mango**
**1 banana**

1 Squeeze the juice from the oranges, measure and make up to 150 ml (1/4 pint) with water.
2 Halve the passion-fruit, scoop out the seeds and add to the orange juice.
3 Quarter the peach and nectarine, remove the stones and cut each quarter into three slices. Add to the orange juice.
4 Peel the mango. Cut the flesh from the stone, cutting carefully down each side to keep the flesh in slices. Dice the flesh and add to the salad.
5 Leave the fruit salad for several hours in the refrigerator to allow the flavours to mellow.
6 No more than 2 hours before serving, peel and slice the banana, add to the salad and mix well.
7 Remove from the refrigerator 30 minutes before serving.

SERVES: 4
PREPARATION & COOKING TIME: 25 minutes
FREEZING: recommended

# BLACKCURRANT KISSEL

Kissels are **traditional Russian desserts** made with soft fruit. This blackcurrant version is my favourite, but create your own with other fruits. Kissel can be served warm or cold.

PER SERVING: 151 calories, 1 g fat

**450 g (1 lb) fresh or thawed frozen blackcurrants**
**55 g (2 oz) light soft brown sugar**
**2 teaspoons grated orange zest**
**juice of 1 orange**
**4 tablespoons red wine or blackcurrant juice mixed with water**
**1–1½ tablespoons arrowroot**
**3 tablespoons cold water**
**1 tablespoon caster sugar**
**1 tablespoon flaked almonds, toasted**

1. Place the blackcurrants, sugar, orange zest, juice and wine in a pan on a low heat. Cover and slowly bring to the boil. Simmer for about 10 minutes or until the fruit is just tender.
2. Mix the arrowroot with the cold water to make a smooth paste; if the fruit has created a lot of juice use the larger amount of arrowroot. Stir the paste into the fruit and simmer gently, stirring constantly until the mixture thickens.
3. Pour into a serving dish and sprinkle with a little caster sugar to prevent a skin forming on the top.
4. Sprinkle the almonds over the kissel.

SERVES: 4
PREPARATION & COOKING TIME:
30 minutes + 45 minutes cooking
FREEZING: not recommended

# LEMON & RASPBERRY DELIGHT

The lemon mixture separates into the **lightest of sponges** with a lemon sauce underneath that combines with the raspberries to make a delightful dessert. I like it best served warm but it can be made in advance and served at room temperature. Vary the fruit by using the same amount of strained, lightly stewed, sweetened rhubarb or gooseberries.

PER SERVING: 224 calories, 6 g fat

**225 g (8 oz) fresh or thawed frozen raspberries**
**25 g (1 oz) soft spread (see page 10)**
**110 g (4 oz) caster sugar**
**grated zest and juice of 1 lemon**
**25 g (1 oz) plain flour**
**150 ml (5 fl oz) skimmed milk**
**1 egg, separated + 1 egg white**

1. Preheat the oven to Gas Mark 4/electric oven 180°C/fan oven 160°C. Prepare a bain-marie (a roasting tin half filled with cold water is ideal).
2. Spoon the raspberries over the base of an ovenproof dish.
3. Cream together the spread, half the sugar and the lemon zest.
4. Mix together the remaining sugar with the flour.
5. Beat the lemon juice into the creamed mixture. The mixture will curdle.
6. Whisk together the milk and the egg yolk. Gradually beat this into the creamed mixture, alternating it with the flour mixture. The mixture will remain curdled.
7. Using a clean whisk, whisk the egg whites together until soft peaks just hold.
8. Fold the egg whites into the lemon mixture. Pour the mixture over the raspberries.
9. Place the dish into the bain-marie and then put that in the middle of the oven. Bake for about 45 minutes, until it is golden brown and the top is set.

SERVES: 6
PREPARATION & COOKING TIME:
25 minutes + 1 hour cooking
FREEZING: not recommended

PER SERVING: 273 calories, 11 g fat

Almost everyone loves this **traditional dessert**, which conjures images of summer days. Pavlova need not be decadent: choose your filling according to the tastes you enjoy and the varying fat contents. Other fruits can be used, try green and black grapes with mandarins in the winter.

FOR THE PAVLOVA:
**3 egg whites**
**175 g (6 oz) caster sugar**
**¼ teaspoon vanilla essence**
**½ teaspoon lemon juice or wine vinegar**
**2 teaspoons cornflour**

FOR THE FILLING:
**425 ml (15fl oz) half-fat crème fraîche, half-fat Greek yogurt or natural fromage frais (not low fat)**

FOR THE TOPPING:
**500 g (1 lb 2 oz) strawberries, sliced if large**

1. Ensure your mixing bowl and whisk are free from grease by washing in very hot soapy water and drying on a clean tea towel. This will help produce a good meringue mixture.
2. Grease a baking sheet and cover with a sheet of baking parchment (or use greaseproof paper and grease the top of it). If it helps, draw a circle 20 cm (8 inches) in diameter on the paper.
3. Preheat the oven to Gas Mark 2/electric oven150°C/fan oven 130°C.
4. Place the egg whites in the bowl and whisk until they are very stiff and the mixture holds firm peaks when the whisk is taken out.
5. Add the caster sugar 1 tablespoon at a time, whisking well between each addition. Carefully fold in the vanilla essence, lemon juice or vinegar and cornflour.
6. Spoon the meringue on to the lined baking sheet to form a 20 cm (8 -inch) circle, piling the mixture up around the edge to form a shell. Bake for an hour until the meringue is a pale biscuit colour with a crisp outside and a marshmallow texture inside. Leave it to cool on the baking sheet.
7. Remove the paper when cold; a pavlova meringue usually cracks a little as it cools. At this stage it can be stored for 2–3 days in an airtight container.
8. Place the pavlova on a flat serving dish. Fill with your choice of filling and pile the strawberries on top.

# STRAWBERRY PAVLOVA

SERVES: 5
PREPARATION & COOKING TIME:
20 minutes + 1 hour cooking
FREEZING: recommended

# BRAMLEY APPLE GINGERBREAD

Gingerbread is relatively low in fat, so makes an ideal topping for a warming winter pudding made with our British Bramley apples. Serve with natural low fat yogurt or custard made with skimmed milk.

PER SERVING: 237 calories, 5 g fat

**450 g (1 lb) Bramley apples**
**1 tablespoon lemon juice**
**1 tablespoon sugar**
**65 g (2½ oz) golden syrup**
**40 g (1½ oz) light soft brown sugar**
**40 g (1½ oz) soft spread (see page 10)**
**110 g (4 oz) plain flour**
**½ teaspoon bicarbonate of soda**
**1 teaspoon ground ginger**
**1 egg**
**2½ tablespoons skimmed milk**

1. Peel, core and slice the apples and toss in the lemon juice to prevent them from browning. Add the spoonful of sugar. Spoon into an ovenproof dish.
2. Preheat the oven to Gas Mark 3/electric 170°C/fan oven 150°C.
3. Put the syrup, brown sugar and soft spread into a saucepan and place over a low heat until the spread has melted. Do not allow the mixture to boil. Stir to mix together and leave to cool.
4. Sieve the flour, bicarbonate of soda and ginger into a mixing bowl.
5. Beat the egg and add the milk to it.
6. Make a well in the centre of the dry ingredients and pour in the liquid ingredients. Mix well to form a smooth batter.
7. Spoon the gingerbread over the apples. Place the dish on a baking sheet. Bake in the centre of the oven for about 1 hour, until a skewer inserted in the centre of the cake mix comes out clean. If the top starts to get too brown, cover loosely with a piece of foil.

SERVES: 4
PREPARATION & COOKING TIME:
40 minutes + 30 minutes cooking
FREEZING: not recommended

# LITTLE FIG & ORANGE COUSCOUS PUDDINGS

These light little puddings are an ideal end to a winter meal. Vary the flavours to suit your tastes: apricot and orange or date and apple juice are both good. Fresh orange juice gives a better flavour than the concentrated variety.

PER SERVING: 174 calories, 1 g fat

**110 g (4 oz) ready-to-eat dried figs, chopped**
**475 ml (17 fl oz) fresh orange juice**
**100 g (3 ½ oz) couscous**
**½ teaspoon ground dried coriander**
**low fat natural yogurt or low fat Greek yogurt, to serve**

1. Prepare a steamer so that it is hot when the puddings are ready.
2. Put the figs and orange juice into a pan, bring to the boil and then cover and simmer for 3 minutes.
3. Meanwhile, grease four individual heatproof moulds, cups or ramekins.
4. Remove half the fruit with a slotted spoon and divide this between the moulds.
5. Add the couscous and coriander to the remaining fruit and juice. Bring back to the boil, turn off the heat and cover. Leave to stand for 10 minutes.
6. Divide the couscous mixture between the moulds and cover tightly with foil.
7. Steam for 30 minutes. Tip from the moulds on to individual plates and serve with low fat natural yogurt or low fat Greek yogurt.

SERVES: 4
PREPARATION & COOKING TIME: 20 minutes
FREEZING: not recommended

# FRESH PINEAPPLE WITH MAPLE SYRUP

Impress your guests with this wonderful combination of flavours, which is so quick and easy to make. Serve with low fat natural or low fat Greek yogurt.

PER SERVING: 155 calories, 0 g fat

**1 pineapple**
**2 teaspoons arrowroot**
**1–2 tablespoons cold water**
**160 ml (5½ fl oz) maple syrup**

1. Thickly peel the pineapple and cut into four slices, lengthways. Remove the core from the pineapple slices and cut the flesh into bite-sized pieces.
2. Blend together the arrowroot and water.
3. Warm the maple syrup in a frying pan.
4. Add the pineapple to the syrup and heat through for 1–2 minutes.
5. Pour the blended arrowroot into the pan, stirring well. Heat until the syrup clears. Serve immediately.

How lovely to arrive at someone's house and be greeted by the smell of baking! That together with a smile makes a true welcome. Cakes and bakes, so often banned from 'diets', do not have to be unhealthy; it depends on what you put in them. Home-made breads and scones are usually quite low in fat

# CAKES & BAKES

and sugar: if you keep them that way by choosing carefully what you spread on them, they are ideal to have as part of a meal or as a snack. Many cakes can be made with less fat than usual and it is just as easy to make a whisked 'fatless' sponge as a high-fat sandwich cake. So get baking!

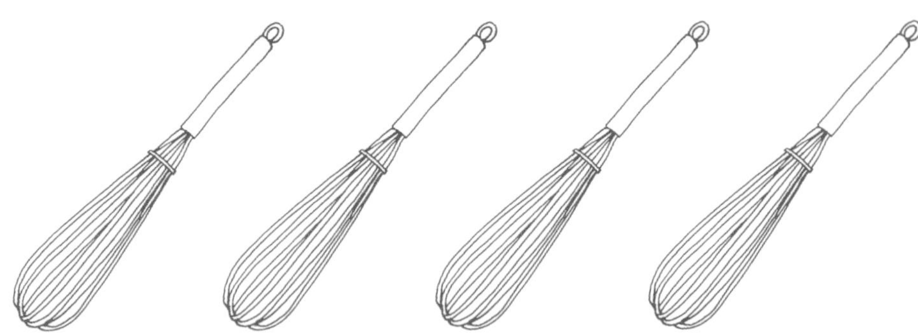

# HONEY CAKE

MAKES: one 15 cm (6 -inch) round cake, giving 8–10 slices
PREPARATION & COOKING TIME: 20 minutes + 45 minutes cooking
FREEZING: recommended

PER SERVING: 146 calories, 5 g fat

If you can keep this cake for 3 days before eating it will taste even better and become **slightly sticky**. It could also be cooked in a 450 g (1lb) loaf tin but then might take a little longer to bake.

**125 ml (4 fl oz) clear honey**
**55 g (2 oz) soft spread (see page 10)**
**25 g (1 oz) demerara sugar**
**55 g (2 oz) wholemeal flour**
**55 g (2 oz) white flour**
**½ teaspoon bicarbonate of soda**
**½ teaspoon ground mixed spice**
**40 g (1 ½ oz) sultanas**
**25 g (1 oz) mixed candied peel**
**grated zest of 1 small lemon**
**1 egg, beaten**
**40 ml (1 ½ fl oz) skimmed milk**

1. Preheat the oven to Gas Mark 3/electric oven170°C/fan oven 150°C. Line a 15 cm (6-inch) round cake tin with greaseproof paper.
2. Pour the honey into a saucepan and add the spread and the sugar. Place over a low heat and allow to melt, stirring occasionally. Do *not* allow the mixture to boil. When the honey mixture has melted, remove it from the heat and leave it to cool.
3. Sift the flours, bicarbonate of soda and spice into a mixing bowl. Add the sultanas, peel and lemon zest to the dry ingredients and mix well.
4. Stir the egg and milk into the cooled honey mixture.
5. Make a well in the dry ingredients and pour in the liquid. Stir well until the mixture is a smooth batter.
6. Pour the batter into the tin, place in the oven and bake for 45 minutes or until the centre is firm when pressed lightly.
7. After 5 minutes, remove from the tin and leave to cool on a wire rack. When cold, wrap in greaseproof paper, place in an airtight container and keep for 3 days before eating.

# PLAITED DATE SLICE

SERVES: 10
PREPARATION & COOKING TIME:
25 minutes + proving + 20 minutes cooking
FREEZING: recommended

PER SERVING: 150 calories, 2 g fat

A wonderfully moist bread, which **can be served in place of cake**. It is delicious warm or cold. Try using other dried fruits in place of the dates; apricots or a mixture of peaches and pineapple would work well. This is a very small quantity of bread to make so you could double it and have one to eat and one to freeze.

**225 g (8 oz) strong plain flour**
**20 g (3/4 oz) soft spread** (see page 10)
**1/2 teaspoon salt**
**1/2 teaspoon sugar**
**1/2 sachet easy-blend dried yeast**
**175 ml (6 fl oz) warm skimmed milk**
**skimmed milk, to glaze**

FOR THE FILLING:
**200 g (7 oz) dates, chopped**
**3 tablespoons lemon juice**
**175 ml (6 fl oz) water**

1. Prepare the dough first. Spoon the flour into a mixing bowl and rub in the spread. Stir in the salt, sugar and yeast. Add most of the warm milk and mix to form a dough, adding the remaining milk if necessary.
2. Knead the dough on the worktop until it feels soft and silky. If necessary, lightly flour the worktop to prevent the dough from sticking.
3. Place the dough in a clean bowl. Cover and leave to prove in a warm place, until the dough has doubled in size.
4. Meanwhile, prepare the filling. Place all the ingredients in a saucepan, bring to the boil and cook gently, uncovered, until the mixture is soft and pulpy. Leave to cool.
5. Lightly grease a baking sheet.
6. When the dough has proved, knock it back with your fist to deflate it and then knead for about 20 seconds. Roll the dough to an oblong, about 35 x 20 cm (14 inches x 8 inches), or adapt the longer length to fit your baking sheet.
7. Place the rolled-out dough on the baking sheet and mark (do not cut) the dough into three, lengthways. Cut diagonal strips 2.5 cm (1 inch) apart down the two outside panels.
8. Spread the dates over the centre panel. Fold the strips alternately over the dates to give a plaited effect.
9. Cover the dough and leave to rise in a warm place for 20–30 minutes. It needs to grow but not lose its shape.
10. Preheat the oven to Gas Mark 7/electric oven 220°C/fan oven 200°C.
11. Brush the plait with milk and place in the oven. Bake for about 20 minutes until golden and cooked. Cover with foil if it starts to get too brown. Leave on the tray for 5 minutes and then transfer to a wire rack.

SERVES: 10–12
PREPARATION & COOKING TIME:
25 minutes + proving + 20 minutes
FREEZING:
recommended (without the icing)

PER SERVING: 210 calories, 3 g fat

# CRANBERRY & ORANGE LOAF

**450 g (1 lb) strong plain flour**
**1 teaspoon salt**
**1 sachet easy-blend dried yeast**
**25 g (1 oz) demerara sugar**
**grated zest of 1 small orange**
**70 g pack of dried cranberries**
**2 tablespoons rapeseed oil or melted soft spread (see page 10)**
**300 ml (10 fl oz) skimmed milk, warmed**

FOR THE ICING:
**80 g (3 oz) icing sugar**
**orange juice, to mix**

1 Spoon the flour, salt, yeast, sugar, most of the orange zest and the cranberries into a bowl and stir to mix. Pour in the fat and most of the warmed milk. Mix to a soft dough, adding more of the milk as required.
2 Knead on a work surface until the dough feels smooth and silky. If necessary, lightly flour the surface to prevent the dough from sticking.
3 Cover the dough and leave to prove in a warm place until doubled in size.
4 Knock the dough down with your fist to deflate it and then shape into a roll and place on a lightly greased baking sheet or put into a large loaftin. Cover and leave to prove again in a warm place for about 25 minutes, until the dough has again approximately doubled in size. The dough will feel springy rather than firm when it is ready.
5 Preheat the oven to Gas Mark 7/220°C/425°F so that it is hot when the bread has proved.
6 Bake for 20–25 minutes or until the base sounds hollow when tapped. If necessary cover the top with foil or dampened greaseproof to prevent excessive browning.
7 Cool on a wire rack.
8 When the loaf is cold, make up the icing. Sift the icing sugar into a basin and very gradually add sufficient juice from the orange to make a thick, pouring icing. Pour over the bread and decorate with the reserved zest.

MAKES: a 20 cm (8 -inch) cake, giving 12–18 slices
PREPARATION & COOKING TIME:
soaking overnight + 20 minutes + 2 hours cooking
FREEZING: recommended

# NOTTINGHAMSHIRE FRUIT CAKE

Most Nottinghamshire WI members are familiar with **'Newark Show Cake'**, a teabread which is made for refreshments at the Show, and many more WI events. I have adapted this recipe, decreasing the sugar and making the fruit element more luxurious, which should take away the need to butter it.

PER SERVING: 254 calories, 6 g fat

**600 g (1 lb 5 oz) luxury mixed dried fruit (including cherries)**
**110 g (4 oz) dried apricots, chopped roughly**
**425 ml (15 fl oz) boiling water**
**110 g (4 oz) soft spread (see page 10)**
**110 g (4 oz) light soft brown sugar, sifted if lumpy**
**1 egg, beaten**
**225 g (8 oz) white self-raising flour**
**225 g (8 oz) wholemeal self-raising flour**

1. Place all the dried fruit in a mixing bowl, pour on the boiling water, cover and leave to soak overnight.
2. The next day, preheat the oven to Gas Mark 3/electric oven 170°C/fan oven 150°C and grease and line a 20 cm (8 -inch) round cake tin.
3. Melt the spread and stir it into the fruit. Mix in the sugar and then the egg. Spoon in both the flours and stir until well mixed.
4. Spoon the mixture into the prepared tin. Make a wide shallow well in the centre. Bake for one hour.
5. Reduce the heat to Gas Mark 2/electric oven 150°C/fan oven 130°C and bake for a further ¾–1 hour or until a skewer inserted into the centre comes out clean. If the cake starts to become too brown, cover it with foil or dampened greaseproof paper.
6. Allow to cool in the tin for about 30 minutes, then remove from the tin and finish cooling on a wire rack.

MAKES: one 1 kg (2 lb) loaf, giving 10–12 slices
PREPARATION & COOKING TIME: 20 minutes + 1¼ hours
FREEZING: recommended

# FRUIT SALAD CAKE

This cake is made in the same way as a teabread and so is **very low in fat**. If you choose to use a spread on it when serving, just choose a very low fat one – or even serve it with natural low fat yogurt. The fruit salad combination is your choice; I used peaches, pears and apricots.

PER SERVING: 204 calories, 4 g fat

**350 g (12 oz) self-raising flour**
**110 g (4 oz) sugar**
**1 egg, beaten**
**90 ml (3 fl oz) milk**
**225 g (8 oz) can of crushed pineapple**
**175 g (6 oz) no-need-to-soak mixed fruits, chopped**
**40 g (1½ oz) soft spread (see page 10), melted**

1. Preheat the oven to Gas Mark 4/electric oven 180°C/fan oven 160°C and grease and line a 1 kg (2 lb) loaf tin.
2. Stir together the flour and sugar.
3. In a separate bowl, mix together the egg, milk, pineapple and juice, mixed fruits and spread.
4. Combine the two mixes thoroughly. Spoon into the prepared tin and bake for 1¼ hours or until a skewer inserted into the centre comes out clean.
5. Cool in the tin for 5–10 minutes and then turn on to a wire rack to cool.

MAKES: one 1 kg (2 lb) loaf, giving 10–12 slices
PREPARATION & COOKING TIME: 20 minutes + 1 hour cooking
FREEZING: recommended

# BANANA & CARROT CAKE

If you like bananas you will enjoy this **lovely moist cake.**

PER SERVING: 196 calories, 8 g fat

**225 g (8 oz) self-raising flour**
**2 teaspoons baking powder**
**80 g (3 oz) light soft brown sugar**
**110 g (4 oz) carrots, grated finely**
**55 g (2 oz) sultanas or chopped dates (optional)**
**2 eggs, beaten**
**110 g (4 oz) soft spread (see page 10), melted**
**2 ripe bananas, mashed**

1. Preheat the oven to Gas Mark 5/electric oven 190°C/fan oven 170°C and grease and line a 1 kg (2 lb) loaf tin.
2. Sift the flour and baking powder into a mixing bowl. Add the sugar, carrots and sultanas or dates (if used). Mix well.
3. Stir in the eggs, spread and bananas to make a soft dropping consistency.
4. Spoon into the prepared tin and bake for 1 hour, or until a skewer inserted into the centre comes out clean.
5. Cool in the tin for 5 minutes; then turn out to cool on a wire rack.

MAKES: 12 muffins
PREPARATION & COOKING TIME: 15 minutes + 20 minutes
FREEZING: recommended

# CHOCOLATE & ORANGE MUFFINS

These **deliciously light** American muffins are a low fat option – just remember to have only one!

PER SERVING: 170 calories, 7 g fat

**240 g (8½ oz) self-raising flour**
**40 g (1½ oz) cocoa powder**
**1½ teaspoons baking powder**
**110 g (4 oz) light soft brown sugar**
**grated zest and juice of 1 orange**
**85 g (3 oz) soft spread (see page 10), melted and cooled**
**1 egg, beaten**

1. Preheat the oven to Gas Mark 6/electric oven 200°C/fan oven 180°C and place paper muffin tin liners in a 12-hole muffin tin.
2. Sieve the flour, cocoa and baking powder into a mixing bowl. Stir in the sugar. Stir in the orange zest using a fork.
3. Measure the orange juice. Add water to make up to 250 ml (9 fl oz).
4. Stir the soft spread into the egg.
5. Make a well in the centre of the dry ingredients. Pour in both quantities of liquid ingredients and stir until just combined. It is important not to stir too much, otherwise the muffins will not be light. The batter will look lumpy but no dry flour should be visible.
6. Divide the mixture equally between the muffin cases.
7. Bake for about 20 minutes, until the tops are firm and they spring back when pressed lightly. Cool on a wire rack.

# LEMON SPONGE WITH A BLUEBERRY FILLING

MAKES: one 19 cm (7-inch) round cake, giving 10 slices
PREPARATION & COOKING TIME: 35 minutes
FREEZING: recommended

PER SERVING: 115 calories, 2 g fat

A true sponge with no added fat makes **a deliciously light and guilt-free cake**. The blueberry filling is made with about half the amount of sugar used to make jam and so balances the sweetness of the cake, but traditional jam or conserve could be used. The spread can be made ahead and will store in the refrigerator for three weeks. The cake should be eaten as fresh as possible as it has little fat to help it keep. For added luxury, spread reduced-fat Greek yogurt in the centre, as well as the fruit.

FOR THE FILLING:
**175 g (6 oz) blueberries**
**2 tablespoons water**
**55 g (2 oz) sugar**

FOR THE CAKE:
**55 g (2 oz) plain flour**
**25 g (1 oz) cornflour**
**3 eggs**
**85 g (3 oz) caster sugar**
**grated zest of 1 lemon**
**1 tablespoon lemon juice**
**1 teaspoon icing sugar for the top (optional)**

1. Make the filling. Place the blueberries in a pan with the water. Bring to the boil and simmer for about 5 minutes, until the fruit is soft.
2. Add the sugar and stir until it has dissolved. Return to the boil and allow to cook, uncovered, at a rolling boil for 8 minutes. This mixture will be very hot and may splash. Remove from the heat and allow to cool. It should have a spreading consistency when cool.
3. Preheat the oven to Gas Mark 4/electric oven 180°C/fan oven 160°F. Prepare two 17–18 cm (6½–7 -inch) sandwich tins: grease the inside edges very thoroughly and line the bases with greaseproof paper.
4. Sift together the flour and cornflour.
5. In a separate bowl, whisk the eggs until foamy. Add the sugar and whisk with the eggs until the mixture is pale and a trail of mixture left by the whisk can be seen for 3 seconds. With a hand-held electric whisk, this will takes 4–5 minutes.
6. Sprinkle the zest over the mixture and re-sift the flour over that. Very gently fold the zest and flour into the whisked mixture. When it is nearly mixed in, sprinkle the lemon juice over and continue folding until no flour can be seen.
7. Immediately pour the mixture into the tins. Tip the tins to level out the mixture; do not spread it with a knife.
8. Place on the middle shelf in the oven straight away and bake for 15 minutes, or until the cakes are golden in colour and have slightly shrunk away from the sides of the tin and the mixture springs back when pressed lightly in the centre.
9. Allow to cool in the tins for 3 or 4 minutes. Check that the edges of the sponges are free from the sides of the tins and turn out. Peel away the greaseproof paper, place it on top of a wire rack and place the sponges base-down on the paper.
10. When both the cake and the filling are cool, place one of the cakes, top-down, on a plate. Spread this with as much of the blueberry spread as you like. Place the other cake on the spread, base-down. If liked. sprinkle a little icing sugar on the top before serving

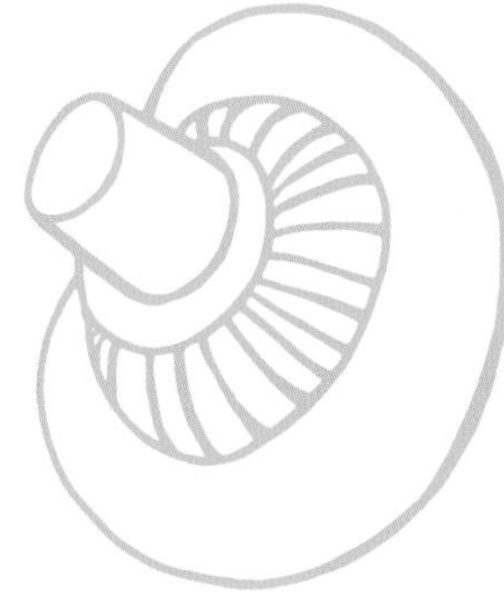

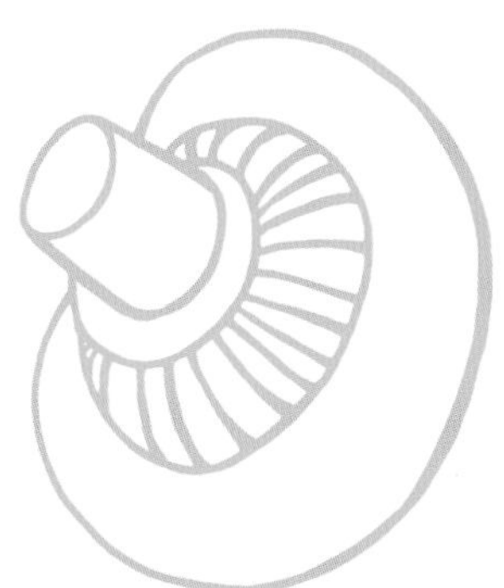

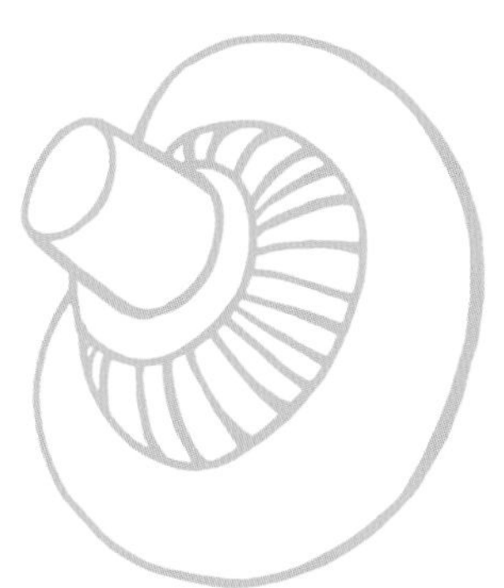